IMAGES
of America

APPLETON

This photograph of College Avenue in downtown Appleton is looking west from Oneida Street. On the south side (left) the Zuelke building is visible on the corner of College and Oneida Street. The first Zuelke building burned in 1928. The seven-story Zuelke building visible in this photograph was completed in 1931. Businesses on the south side of College Avenue included Morris Lea Furs, Brettschneider Furniture, and Wichman's Furniture Company in the distance. Businesses on the north side of College Avenue (right side) included Montgomery Ward, Millers, Fred Hopkins Drugs, Pettibone Peabody, Campbell's, the Elite Theatre, and Aid Association for Lutherans. (Image courtesy of Dave Kalz.)

ON THE COVER: This view, taken during the summer of about 1925 in downtown Appleton on College Avenue west of Appleton Street, shows the street lined with decorations and residents watching the grand parade. The Appleton Police Department is shown on horses for the Fourth of July parade. (Image courtesy of Arne Nettekoven.)

IMAGES
of America

APPLETON

Appleton Historical Society

ARCADIA
PUBLISHING

Published by Arcadia Publishing
Charleston, South Carolina

Library of Congress Control Number: 2014958791

For all general information, please contact Arcadia Publishing:
Telephone 843-853-2070
Fax 843-853-0044
E-mail sales@arcadiapublishing.com
For customer service and orders:
Toll-Free 1-888-313-2665

Visit us on the Internet at www.arcadiapublishing.com

*To all the local Appleton historians who saved their family
photographs and shared their memories of Appleton*

CONTENTS

ACKNOWLEDGMENTS

Images of America: *Appleton* was a journey that had many contributors. There were people who submitted pictures, captions, interest, personal knowledge, and more. I would like to thank my fellow Appleton Historical Society board members who supported my desire to do this book: Tom Sutter, Dave Buss, Jim Richter, Laura Leimer, Brian Schneider, Christine Williams, Linda Muldoon, Karen Probst, Mark Moderson, and Jim Krueger.

I would like to thank all the photograph and caption contributors: Dave Buss, Kay Forton, Carol McIntyre, John Marx, Michael Broeren, Dave Kalz, Laura Leimer, Tom Sutter, Barbara Hirn, Christine Williams, Joanne Clark, the Malcow family, Jim Krueger, the Ken Weiland family, We Energies, Mark Moderson, the Ken and Helen Schmidt family, the Caroline Koester Staedt family, Bruce Pollard, the Schwahn family, John McFadden, Bob Kohl, Phil Grishaber, Raymond Noffke, Jon Porter, Mary Schulz, the Walter and Irene Koester family, the Vogt family, Gretchen Hauert, the Christensen family, the Jacobs family, the Steidl family, Rosemarie DeBruin, Steve Smits, the Joan V. Hurley family, Joan Giulliani, Paul Heid, the Tom Butler family, Sheila Brucks, Dave and Barb Daelke, Karen Van Lyssal, Kris and Ann Sager, Clarice Belling, Joe Gaerthofner, Walter and Mickey Schmidt, Allan Wrobel, Gary Schierl, Paul Hinzman, and Ike Spangenberg.

I would like to thank Karen Probst and Diana Sandberg for providing access to the library's photographs and much-appreciated scanning, Lawrence University archivist Erin Dix, City of Appleton utilities director Chris Shaw; Appleton Police Department historian Arne Nettekoven, Wisconsin Electric and Doc Musekamp, First Congregational Church, the Monte Alverno Capuchins, the Hearthstone Historic House Museum—Stephanie Malaney, Ann Kloehn, and Antoinette Powell—the Moses Montifiore Congregation, BMO Bank and Douglas Paschen, Hoffman Corporation, and the History Museum at the Castle and chief curator Nick Hoffman (who more than once answered my where, when, and what questions.).

I would like to thank my husband, Joe Sargeant, who poured over maps of the ever-changing Fox River islands and banks with me; my children, Joey, Helen, and Paul; my mom, Kay Forton, who submitted photographs, scanned, and more; and my father, Paul Hinzman, who let us use his house as a scanning hub to get it all done. I would also like to thank my editor, Jesse Darland, for keeping me on track, editing, and helping me craft the layout.

Unless otherwise noted, all images appear courtesy of the Appleton Historical Society, and all captions are by Gwen Sargeant.

Very truly,

Gwen Sargeant

INTRODUCTION

This work is a celebration of the history of Appleton. It includes Lawrence University, the Fox River, electricity, people, businesses, public service, sports, dance, food, drinks, and celebrations. The process of creating this book began as an idea at a board meeting of the Appleton Historical Society and developed into a yearlong adventure into the depths of residents' personal collections. There were scanning events, quiet conversations at Appleton Historical Society public meetings, and big announcements ("We need your pictures!").

This book is an opportunity to see Appleton as it was in the earliest of days and to travel down College Avenue as it becomes the place it is today. The ever-changing Fox River was of special interest as it was dammed and shaped to suit the needs of a growing community.

Chapter One includes the beginnings of Appleton, which are inextricably tied to the "University in the Woods," Lawrence Institute. Amos Lawrence, a well-known philanthropist of the 19th century, planned for a Methodist institution in the new territory of Wisconsin. Reeder Smith, H.L. Blood, and George Day formed a committee to find a home for the Lawrence Institute. In 1874, J. Alfred Dull wrote the following:

> In the month of May, 1846 a solitary horseman was pursuing his way from Green Bay to Oshkosh. He had passed beyond the thinly settled regions of the French claims and all about him now was primeval nature. He stood upon the edge of a large plateau. Grand old trees stretched far away on either hand. Before him, broad and deep, between high green banks, rolled the clear waters of the Fox River to where they poured their vast volume over a natural fall. It was a scene fit to inspire an artist mind with the deepest enthusiasm, and to call beautiful visions to the imagination of the poet. Although, he was fully conscious of the rare beauty of the site our horseman, being neither poet nor artist, took a more utilitarian view of the prospect before him; upon his mind it indelibly impressed itself as a most perfect position for a city.

Henry Levake Blood was that solitary horseman. He gazed upon what would eventually become the city of Appleton.

Chapter Two is a trip down the Fox River, the heart and soul of Appleton. The river brought the early settlers to the area and also sustained them with waterpower that spawned many business ventures in the early days: flour mills, barrel and sash making, and planning. The "flats" included the north and south banks of the river and the north and south islands. Over the years, many mills began service on the river, including the Conkey Flour Mill, the Atlas Mill, Vulcan Mill, and the Woolen Mill.

Chapter Three showcases Appleton's hydroelectric history. "Bright as day" was the description given to the light of the first Edison dynamo–lit buildings. According to the golden jubilee anniversary celebration souvenir booklet, "It was on Saturday night, September 30th, 1882, that the world's first water driven electrical station was placed in successful operation at Appleton,

Wisconsin. This fact was dually reported in the weekly newspapers of the time. The people of Appleton went to see light in those early fall evenings and marveled, declaring them to be as 'bright as day.'" Today, we know it as the nation's first hydroelectric station.

Chapter Four includes the first churches in Appleton, many of which share the same story of small beginnings. The first sermon in Appleton was delivered by the Reverend William K. Sampson at the J.F. Johnston Shanty. The congregations began in little wooden buildings or storefronts, with only a few members, and they grew to inhabit large, beautiful buildings with thousands of members.

Chapter Five is a look at Appleton's many different businesses of every type and size. In 1855, area merchants included Theodore Conkey, C.G. Adkins, W.S. Warner, White and Carhart, Buck and Hawley, McCoughney, Lite, and Willy. According to J.A. Dahl, "The total sales of merchandise during that year amounted to $160,000." There were banks: First National, Appleton State Bank, and more. There were laborers, craftsmen, artisans, insurance men, hotelkeepers, dentists, doctors, fruit sellers, and retailers of all sorts. The city grew at a quick pace as new settlers joined the pioneers. By 1887, there were well over 500 businesses flourishing in Appleton.

Chapter Six is a testament to Appleton's many rich traditions of merriment. Appleton's mix of English, German, French, Creole, and Irish early inhabitants led to many businesses. In 1874, there were four saloons, two breweries, three bakeries, two meat markets, and three cigar makers. A half century later, in 1924, there were 7 bakeries, 11 confectioners, 17 meat markets, 6 cigar makers, as well as 3 soda bottlers, 11 restaurants, and 6 fruit sellers. Note that in 1924 there were no saloons and no breweries; it was Prohibition, and one needed the password to find out where those were located.

Chapter Seven presents the beauty of Appleton's residences, parks, and leisure activities. The early homes of Appleton were nothing more than wooden shanties. When industry began to take hold along the river; the money began to flow as well. The homes became more grand and ornate, and the hotels added romantic details and luxury to the once rustic, pioneer Appleton. The city had parks and squares throughout, with the original ravine areas made some of the best parks with their hidden, private, sanctuary-like atmosphere. Lutz Park once boasted a ski jump, and Jones Park still hosts a winter skating rink.

Chapter Eight tours many places in Appleton's public school system. Carolyn Kellogg surmises in her book A History of Pride, Appleton Public Schools that Daniel Huntley was the first teacher in the winter of 1851. He taught at the southeast corner of College Avenue and Oneida Street in a "rude frame building." William K. Sampson was the first superintendent of schools. A century later, in 1951, the school district had grown to seven elementary schools, two junior high schools, and one high school. The schools expanded rapidly with the increase in population.

Chapter Nine demonstrates public service throughout Appleton's history. Many citizens experienced the motions of getting ready for war. Appleton community members lead the charge to form a company of men for the Civil War. Many people represented Appleton in Company G. During both world wars, many citizens served, leaving behind many families to hang the flag. Appleton is served by many public-service professions, including postal workers and the fire, police, and other city departments.

Chapter Ten highlights the delightful history of celebrations, music, and sports in Appleton. Appleton hosted many early baseball teams, great shows, radio personalities, and parades. The circus parade made several trips to town, thrilling residents. Appleton is still known for great parades, including the Christmas parade and Flag Day parade. This book is a starting point. It is a snapshot of pieces of Appleton's rich, historical rise on the bluff. Many of the captions in the book include the geographical details to lead around the city. One might still find that spot on the bluff where the Fox River can be seen as it was in 1846.

One

FOUNDERS AND LAWRENCE UNIVERSTIY

Main Hall at Lawrence University was built in 1853–1854, as the institution was growing from a preparatory school to a college proper. In its early years, Main Hall housed classrooms, the library, faculty and administrative offices, a chapel, and a men's dormitory. Today, it is the oldest building on campus and the only one in the National Register of Historic Places. Despite persistent rumors, there is no evidence suggesting that Main Hall served as a stop on the Underground Railroad. It did, however, serve as a gathering place during the Civil War, with lectures and aid coordination for families of soldiers taking place there. (Image courtesy of Lawrence University; caption provided by Erin Dix.)

Amos Adams Lawrence (1814–1886) of Boston orchestrated the founding of Lawrence University on lands he owned in Wisconsin, pledging $10,000 to endow the school on the condition that Wisconsin Methodists match the sum. The charter for Lawrence Institute of Wisconsin was granted by the Territorial Legislature on January 15, 1847. By the time classes began on November 12, 1849, the school's name had changed to Lawrence University. The village of Appleton (named for Amos Lawrence's wife, Sarah Appleton Lawrence) grew up around the school. (Image courtesy of Lawrence University; caption provided by Erin Dix.)

Rev. Reeder Smith (1804–1892), a Methodist clergyman, served as Amos Lawrence's agent in negotiating the deal to purchase the land for Lawrence University. He also assisted with fundraising efforts and served as general agent for the fledgling university until 1849. (Image courtesy of the Appleton Public Library; caption provided by Erin Dix.)

Plan of the Three Village Plats of Grand Chute, Appleton-Lawesburgh, Outagamie County, Wis.

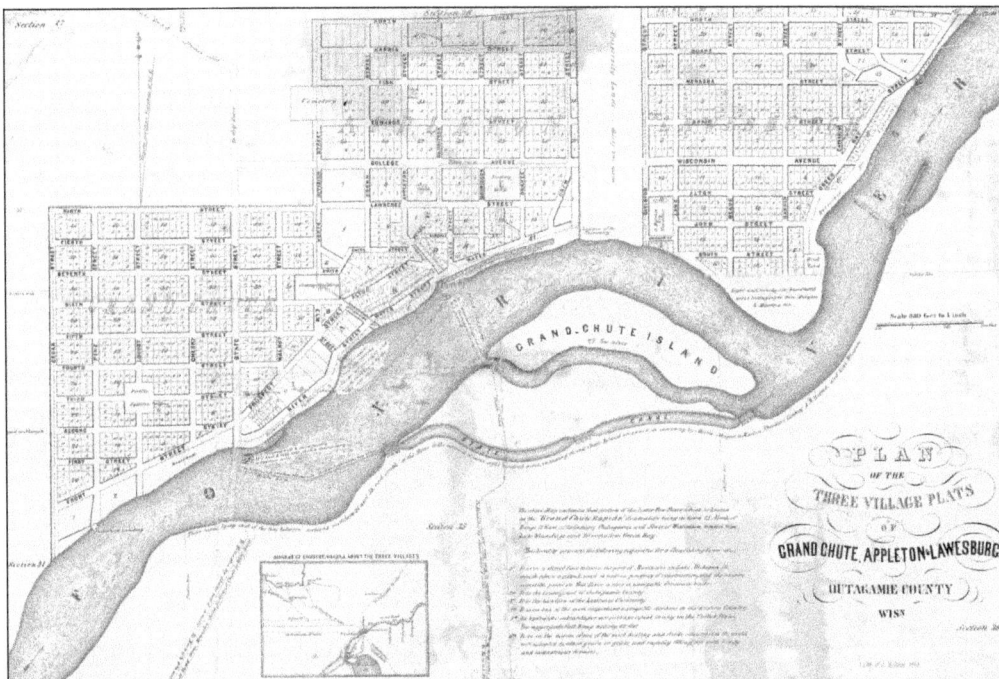

In 1853, Appleton consisted of three separate village plats: Grand Chute (originally known as Martin), Appleton, and Lawesburgh. These made up the west, center, and east sections of the eventual city of Appleton. The sections were divided by deep ravines that crossed the landscape from the river inward. This map was given to Mary F. Mead by Mrs. Perry Smith on April 28, 1853. Mary Mead subsequently gave it to Maggie Grignon, who gave it to the Appleton Public Library in 1924. The map includes a number of interesting and outdated street names. Streets in Appleton were named for Lawrence donors, family members, trees, Native American words, and numbers. In 1857, the three plats were joined, and the city of Appleton was formed. Amos Story was the first mayor. (Image courtesy of the Appleton Public Library.)

Rev. William Harkness Sampson (1808–1902) came to the Wisconsin Territory in 1842, where he worked as a Methodist minister. He was named presiding elder of the Green Bay Mission District in 1844. While serving in this position, he was approached by Amos Lawrence's agents to assist with the founding of Lawrence University. He served as the principal and primary financial agent of Lawrence University from the opening of classes in 1849 until 1853, during the time that the institution operated only as a preparatory school. (Image courtesy of Lawrence University; caption provided by Erin Dix.)

Lawrence University was founded as a coeducational institution in 1847 and opened its doors to preparatory students in 1849. By 1853, some students were ready to begin college-level work. The first class of four men and three women graduated four years later, in 1857. The three women are, from left to right, Francena Kellogg Buck, Adelaide Grant Carver, and Lucinda Darling Colman. In the men's portrait, the man seated at left is Henry Colman. The others, in no particular order, are Allen Jeffrey Atwell, Justin Martyr Copeland, and William Dolphin Storey. (Images courtesy of Lawrence University; caption provided by Erin Dix.)

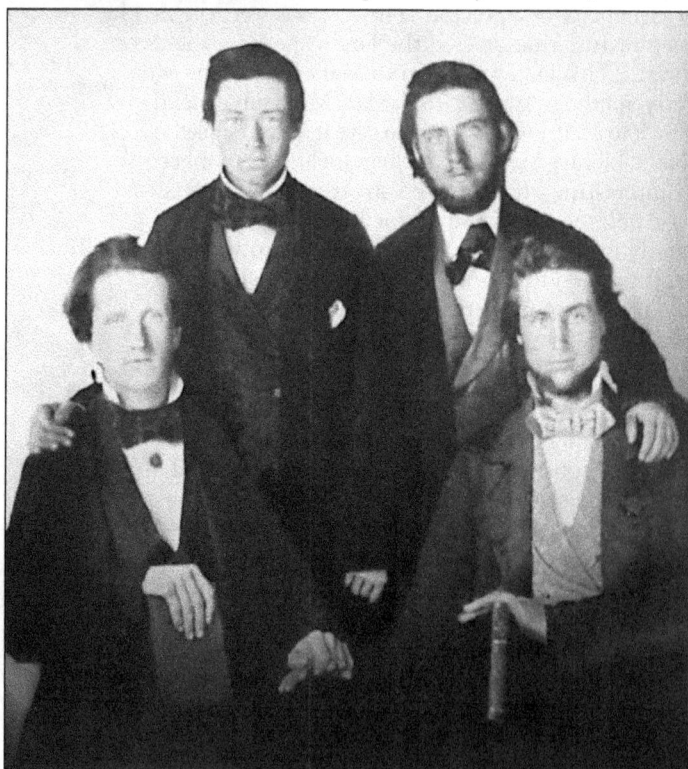

The view from College Avenue and Oneida Street to the northwest included two churches and a school. The leftmost church steeple is the Episcopal church finished in 1866 on the corner of Appleton and Edwards (now Washington) Streets. The church on the right with the pointed steeple is the First Baptist Church, located on the corner of Appleton and Fisk (now Franklin) Streets. The school across the street from First Baptist was known as the Hercules School. (Image courtesy of the History Museum at the Castle.)

The view from the north side of College Avenue looking southwest includes the south side of College Avenue between Morrison and Oneida Streets. The background shows the First Congregational Church, which was known as "the Little Brown Church," located on South Oneida Street between College Avenue and Lawrence Street. The lot for the church was a donation from Amos Lawrence, and services began there in 1853. (Image courtesy of the History Museum at the Castle.)

College Avenue in 1868 was a dirt road, cleared of stumps, that many a horse and wagon negotiated. The south side of College Avenue (left) includes a coffins and furniture dealer, harness makers, and mercantile shops. The photograph looks west from an area between Oneida and Morrison Streets and includes the Johnston House (right foreground). The Johnstons kept a hotel in Appleton, and their support was integral to the building of the community. The building on the north side also included several local druggists and the "Red Coat" dry goods and grocery. (Image courtesy of the Appleton Public Library.)

The first steps to building the Lawrence Chapel began in 1908 when $5,000 was pledged in the memory of Helen Fairfield Naylor. Together with previous contributions from Myra Plantz, this amount began a campaign to construct the chapel. The plan was not realized until 1917, when a large, anonymous donation from an Appleton citizen set the construction underway. The chapel was finished in 1919 and dedicated to Helen Naylor and Myra Plantz. Located at 504 East College Avenue, it has 1,184 seats and is used for concerts, convocations, and community events. (Image courtesy of John Marx.)

Students stacked large blocks of ice to build this chapel in 1933. Ice sculptures were a part of the Winter Carnival, a tradition at Lawrence University. The Winter Carnival included activities such as broomball and tug-of-war, and sometimes, if the weather did not cooperate, students played games indoors by the fire in the Memorial Union Hearth. (Image courtesy of Laura Leimer.)

This 1932 aerial view of the Lawrence University campus was taken by Lt. R.C. Wriston. The photograph includes the Memorial Chapel (left foreground) and the Main Hall (upper center) with its cupola. On the river (background), the buildings include the Underwood Observatory (domed), the campus gym, Stephenson Science Hall, and Orsmby Hall. (Image courtesy of Lawrence University; caption provided by Erin Dix.)

On April 22, 1936, as part of a nationwide antiwar demonstration, 700 students from Lawrence College intended to march down College Avenue. Though the Appleton Police Department had initially granted permission for the parade, they revoked it shortly before it began. When one student attempted to cross the line at the corner of College Avenue and Drew Street, he was clubbed by police. The incident gained national media attention. (Image courtesy of Lawrence University; caption provided by Erin Dix.)

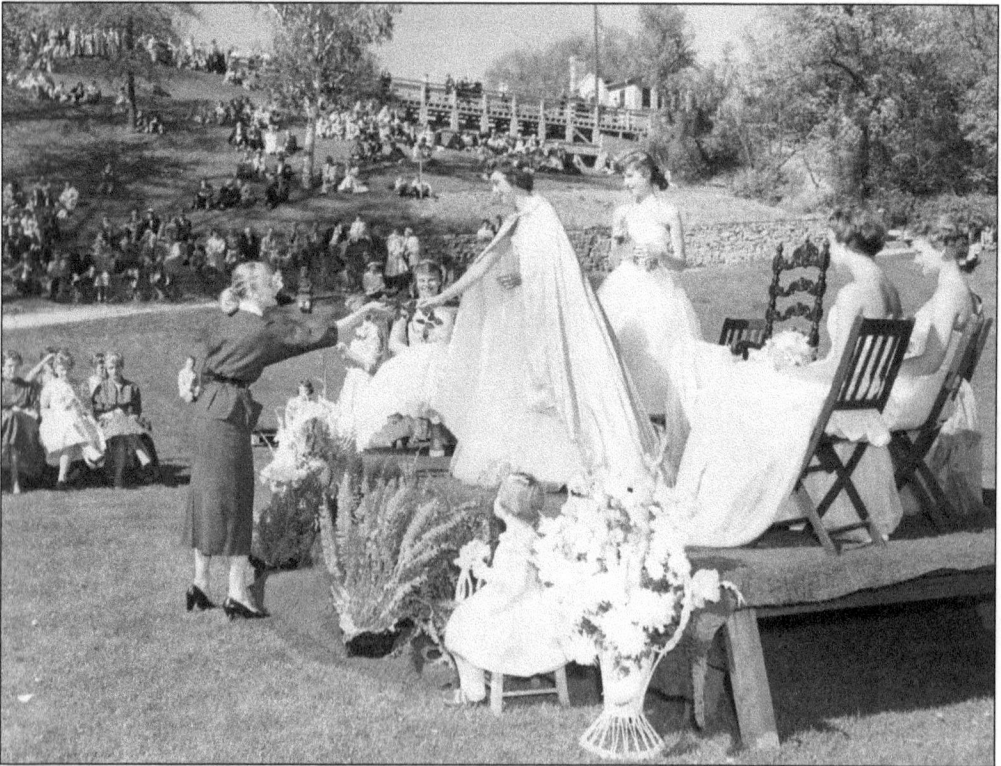

May queen Helen Williams, Lawrence College class of 1955, accepts her crown from Barbara Randall, class of 1956, at the 1955 May Day celebration on the hill below the Memorial Union. May Day celebrations were a spring tradition at Lawrence from 1906 to 1966. (Image courtesy of Lawrence University; caption provided by Erin Dix.)

Two

Engines of the Industrial Fox River

Here is the steamboat *B.F. Carter* coming through Lock No. 3 near Lawe Street in Appleton. The Carter, a sternwheeler, was built in Oshkosh in 1876 and ran until 1912. Measuring 110 feet by 24 feet, it plied the waters of Lake Winnebago and the Lower Fox River during the heyday of the steamboats on the Fox River. This image, from a glass lantern slide, was also used for a postcard in the early 1900s. In recent years, the Fox River has experienced a resurgence as the canals and locks have been refurbished. Folks can once again experience the beauty and mystery of a trip on this stretch of river where Marquette and Joliet passed in 1673. (Image and caption courtesy of Tom Sutter.)

A three-mast schooner carrying a cargo of logs docked in Appleton's first lock in about 1885. The 275-mile river system that includes the Fox and Lower Wisconsin Rivers extends from Lake Michigan to the Mississippi River. Beginning in the 1820s, the Fox River began to be viewed as direct water highway to the West, but the strong current and rapids on the Lower Fox River made boat traffic impossible. The solution was to build a series of dams, locks, and canals, bypassing the river's obstacles and allowing for safe navigation. Construction began in 1851, and over the course of three decades, 26 hand-operated locks were constructed. In the distance are Appleton Paper and Pulp Company and Kimberly-Clark's Tioga, Vulcan, and Atlas Paper Mills. (Image courtesy of Joanne Clark; caption provided by Christine Williams.)

This c. 1950 view shows Appleton's Lock No. 4 from Telulah Park. An approaching barge or boat prompted service to the hand-operated locks with its whistle. To provide an around-the-clock response, the US Corps of Engineers constructed modest government houses adjacent to the locks where the lockmasters and their families could reside. Families adjusted to the unique life on the locks. With the river as their backyard, they had easy access to boating, fishing, and swimming. In winter, there was ice fishing, skating, and sledding in the frozen canal. This lock house was located on an island, and the family traversed the narrow lock gates using carts to transport items to the other side. (Image courtesy of the Malcow family; caption provided by Christine Williams.)

This photograph looks north across the Fox River. The center building in the photograph's background is Lawrence Main Hall. The mansion to the left is the Augustas Ledyard Smith home. The buildings in the flats (river level) include the Edison Electric and Gas Company. Beginning in 1882, those buildings housed three Edison dynamos run by the water current of the Fox River. (Image courtesy of the Appleton Public Library.)

At the end of this stone dam on the Fox River is the Appleton Paper and Pulp Company, one of the largest mills in the west. The foreman in 1880 was John Dodd, a papermaker of much experience and well-known skill. It was a stock corporation, and H.J. Rodgers was the treasurer and secretary. Built in 1882, the home of Rodgers appears on the hill beyond the paper mill, in the center of the image. (Image courtesy of Barbara Hirn.)

The Outagamie Mill's original proprietor was W.L. Barteau. He sold to Messrs. Cross and Willy in 1878. Each year, they made many improvements. In 1879, the middling purifiers were put in place, and everything in the mill was overhauled and repaired. In 1881, the mill was destroyed by fire. (Image courtesy of Dave Kalz.)

Theodore Conkey himself erected the Conkey Flour Mill, on the left, in 1853. The mill had three sets of burrs. The mill used the water to drive the large grindstone. Theodore Conkey sold the mill in 1861 to pursue other interests, but he returned to Appleton in 1865 and repurchased his old mill property, adding four more sets of burrs. According to the newspaper, he had one of the best mills in the state, producing up to 60,000 barrels per year. (Image courtesy of the Appleton Public Library.)

The Appleton Woolen Mill (light-colored brick building on right) was the property of Hutchinson & Company. The mill was located on what was known as Grand Chute Island (now North Island) and was engaged in the manufacture of all wool flannels; balmorals; and a variety of knitting yarns. Valley Iron Works is located to the right of the mill. On left, Tellulah Paper Mill can be seen in the distance. (Image courtesy of Michael Broeren.)

In July 1899, the Appleton Toy and Furniture Company began. It was preceded by Union Toy. The company's buildings were powered by water and steam. At its height, the Appleton Toy and Furniture Company had 80 employees and built porch and lawn furniture, children's sleds, chairs, and hobbyhorses known as "shoo flies." The factory was located at the bottom of the Lawe Street hill on the south side of the river. (Image courtesy of Michael Broeren.)

Outagamie Mills, in the center, was built about 1852 and originally made axe handles. M.F. Barteau was the agent in 1865 when it was turned into a flour mill. Barteau arranged for Albert Miller to be the head miller. The mill was capable of producing superfine XX-quality flour. In 1878, Cross and Willy purchased the mill. They added many new pieces of machinery in 1880. (Image courtesy of Dave Kalz.)

The Eagle Manufacturing Company was located in a two-story factory with waterpower in the Second Ward and had the latest improved machinery and foundry. The company eventually moved to 414 Winnebago Street. The agricultural farm implements they built included tractors, Eagle self-reversing hay carriers, single- and double-harpoon forks, and hay tools. In 1921, they kept the plant manufacturing all through the winter because of the high demand of their tractor.

J.F. Atkinson owned the Appleton Chair Factory. The building, which housed a chair and bedstead factory, was located on Grand Chute Island next to the Hutchinson Woolen Mill. Thomas Henry Ryan's *History of Outagamie County* gave details. "In June of 1881, the Hutchinson Woolen Mill and the Atkinson Furniture Factory were destroyed by fire: 200 persons were thrown out of employment; one man, August Bothe, was burned to death, others scorched and hurt and many had narrow escapes. The total loss was estimated at from $75,000 to $100,000. The fire department did its best, but was unequal to a task like this. Engine No. 2 was found to be disabled, when it was presumed to be in a fighting condition."

Riverside Paper Mill was managed by M.T. Boult. The mill was one of the most substantial buildings on the river. Standing four stories high, it was built of heavy timber and brick, with iron shutters and doors. Riverside was "particularly fire proof," which was important in that day and age. The power was furnished by two turbine waterwheels. The C&NR Railroad ran right to the mill.

Negotiations began in the late 1860s to secure a blast furnace for the city of Appleton. In February 1870, with $50,000 and land from Edward West, the blast furnace was built on the North Island. (Image courtesy of the Ken Weiland family.)

According to *Appleton, Wis., Illustrated* (1892), "Valley Iron Works was incorporated in 1882, with capital stock of $50,000, by G. D. Rowell, president; A. L. Smith, vice-president; D. G. Rowell, secretary and treasurer. The company had extensive machine shops and foundry, manufacturing water wheels, pulp grinders, sulfur burners, beating and washing engines, friction clutches, wood splitters, barkers, sawing machines, brass and bronze castings, and general founders. The president, Mr. G. D. Rowell, is an experienced mechanic, and has devised and patented many valuable machines, prominent among which is The Rowell Noiseless Vibrating Screen, for screening pulp and all kinds of paper stock."

This view of the Fox River Valley looks north from the south bank. The far left is Lake Street (now Olde Oneida Street), and the far right is the John Street Bridge. The mills on the South Island are visible. (Image courtesy of Jim Krueger.)

Thilmany Pulp and Paper Company was located at the bottom of the John Street hill on the north side of the river. The mill included turbines powered by the Fox River. The water came in through the head race and went under the building and back out to the Fox River. Papermaker Emil Klein, second from left, retired after a tenure as the Thilmany Mill manager. (Image courtesy of Barbara Hirn.)

Pictured here are Thilmany Paper Mill workers. Mary Mauer Klein (married to Emil Klein) is the second woman from the right in the first row. (Image courtesy of Barbara Hirn.)

The Appleton Hay and Tool Company was located on the river at the bottom of the John Street hill. The John Street wooden bridge was 575 feet long. The men in the photograph are building a stone wall at the end of the bridge. A large piece of stone is suspended in the air, and the horse and wagon are ready to deliver more stone. A bicycle rests against the railing in the foreground. (Image courtesy of Jon Porter.)

Men work on the Lake Street Bridge (now Olde Oneida) in approximately 1890. The trolley tracks hung out over the water, and the men are laying the steel for reinforcement. One man stands with a trowel for the finishing cement. (Image courtesy of Dave Kalz.)

In 1922, work began on the Soldier's and Sailor's Cherry Street Bridge (now Memorial Drive). The crew included John Fisher (the boss), Pat Fisher, and Bill Fisher. (Image courtesy of Mary Schulz.)

The view upriver from the bluff at Lawrence University includes the train bridge and the Lake Street Bridge (now known as the Olde Oneida Street Bridge). The factories to the right include the Riverside Flour Mills, Cross and Willy's Flouring, Hauert and Wamboldt's Flouring Mills, and S.R. Willy's Flour Mill. The mills at the center back include the Atlas Paper Mill and Kimberly Clark and Co. Flouring Mill.

The photograph shows a view from the depot on the island between the US Canal (later known as the Green Bay and Mississippi Channel) and the South Channel. In the foreground is the rail yard, and in the background, the woolen mills. Lawrence University can be seen on the bluff behind the woolen mills. (Image courtesy of the Appleton Public Library.)

From the south bank of the river, looking north across lock No. 4, one can see the Interlake Pulp Mill's lumber stacks. In the background, the dual church steeples from St. Mary's are visible, as is the St. Joseph's steeple on Lawrence Street. The water tower at Walnut Street is located at the rear center of the photograph. At river level, the woolen mills are visible. (Image courtesy of Dave Kalz.)

Three

EDISON AND HYDROELECTRICITY

The Henry Rogers home on the bluff of the Fox River was first in the country lit by hydroelectricity. William Waters, a prominent Fox Valley turn-of-the-century architect, designed the stunning home. Henry J. and Cremora Rogers and their daughter Kitty lived in the home approximately 11 years before leaving Appleton in 1893. The house then changed hands nine times. In the 1930s, it was a public restaurant called the Hearthstone because of its nine fireplaces. In 1986, the City of Appleton considered razing the building. A grassroots group effort by Appleton residents raised enough money to purchase the property in December 1986, saving it from destruction. The group formed the Friends of Hearthstone, Inc., and opened the home as a museum, emphasizing its Edison heritage. The building is being restored to the historical era of 1882 to 1895. (Image courtesy of Bob Kohl; caption provided by the Hearthstone Historic Museum.)

Henry Rogers, superintendent of the Atlas Pulp and Paper Company, had the foresight to get involved in hydroelectricity, which would light the mills as well as his own home. According to Ann Larsen, Henry Rogers wrote to the Western Edison Light Company on November 11, 1882, and said, "Gentlemen, I have used 50 lamps in my residence and have used them about 60 days. I am pleased with them beyond expression and do not see how they can be improved upon. No heat no smoke no vitiated air and the light steady and pleasant in every way and more economical than gas and quite as reliable." (Image courtesy of the Appleton Public Library.)

Kimberly-Clark's Vulcan Paper Mill was built in 1881. To its east was the Atlas Paper Mill, which still stands. The Vulcan Paper Mill was one of three buildings to be lit on September 30, 1882, with the first Edison central hydroelectric power station. This historic lighting event also powered electricity to the Appleton Paper and Pulp Company. The Vulcan Mill produced book paper, while the adjoining Tioga Paper Mill produced print paper and later, book paper. (Caption provided by the Hearthstone Historic Museum.)

This is an interior view of the first three-wire Edison Electric station, built in 1884. The new central station was located on Edison Street on the south island where the Electric Trolley's car barn would eventually stand. Seated in the picture is William Kurz, the station's first superintendent. (Image courtesy of the Ken Weiland family.)

The Waverly House was built of brick and stood four stories high. William Cottrill was in charge of the fine service one would receive upon arrival. The rooms were fit with the finest furnishings, and the cuisine was delightful to the palate. The Waverly House also boasted of being the first electrically lit hotel in the Midwest. It was lit in 1883. (Image courtesy of the Appleton Public Library.)

The second Vulcan electric power plant was located on Vulcan Street. It began operation in November 1882. The Vulcan power plant was located in the clump of three trees to the right of the large building (at center) called the Vulcan Street Blast Furnace. The three trees are covering up the tailrace that ran the water for power through the turbines operating the Edison dynamo. (Image courtesy of the Appleton Public Library.)

The 1932 civic celebration of electric power included an outdoor public meeting at the new Vulcan power station replica. The meeting included music, an address by Mayor Goodland and F.J. Sensenbrenner, and the dedication of the new replica. It was presented by William Kurz, Edward O'Keefe, and Al Langstadt. (Image courtesy of the Grishaber family.)

Augustus Ledyard Smith married Edna Taylor in 1860, and they had two sons. They were members of the First Congregational Church. A.L. Smith began the First National Bank of Appleton in 1870 and was its president until 1891. He was a leader in the Edison Electric Gas and Light Company in Appleton, and he also served as Appleton's mayor. (Image courtesy of the Appleton Public Library.)

The A.L. Smith home, pictured on the corner of Alton and Lawe Streets, was the one of the first homes lit with electricity in Appleton. Electricity was run to the home from the Vulcan Street Station below it on the north island. The Vulcan Station also lit the three mills, the blast furnace, and an additional home belonging to H.D. Smith. (Image courtesy of Mark Moderson.)

The Riverside Cemetery run of the electric streetcar is pictured above. Appleton's electric streetcars ran from August 16, 1886, until April 6, 1930. Below is a run of the streetcar in downtown Appleton. The electric streetcars, horses, and bicycles provided the multimodal transportation in Appleton. (Above image courtesy of the Tom Butler family; below image courtesy of the History Museum at the Castle.)

The bus drivers of Wisconsin Michigan Power Company are pictured dressed in their new uniforms. The company began in 1890 as the Appleton Street Railway Company and was known as Wisconsin Michigan Power Company from 1927 until 1941. The trolley service ran from 1890 to 1930. Pictured in the first row, far left is Herman Kloes, superintendent of transportation. (Image courtesy of Mark Moderson.)

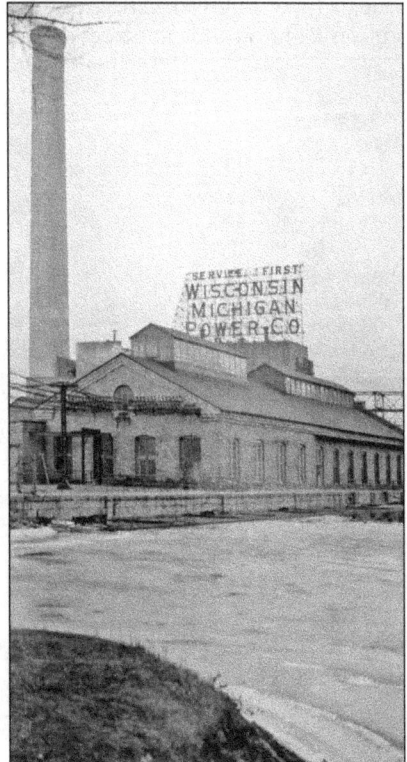

The Wisconsin Michigan Power Company, formerly also known as the Wisconsin Traction, Light, Heat, and Power Company, was located on the north bank of the Fox River (now the below the College Avenue bridge). V.W. Zirke stated, "No less than twenty five cities and villages within 60 miles from Appleton received their light and power from the local plant." (Image courtesy of WE Energies.)

The replica of the Vulcan Street Plant was built in 1932 to commemorate the 50th anniversary of hydroelectric power. The replica was located in front of the Edison Electric building at 825 South Oneida (now Olde Oneida) Street. Today, it stands just feet from the original location of the real Vulcan Plant on Vulcan Street on the North Island. (Image courtesy of the Grishaber family.)

Four

CHURCHES AND WORSHIP

The Presbyterian church was located on the southwest corner of Drew Street and College Avenue. The Reverend Gardner led the service in 1893. Presbyterians were in Appleton as early as the 1850s. Brooks High School classes were held in the Presbyterian Hall located a few doors west of Oneida Street on College Avenue. In 1920, Leo Reid Burrows served as the pastor.

Above, First Congregational Church (now First Congregational United Church of Christ) was the first church building constructed in Appleton (1850). Its founding members were "Yankees" from New England and New York who brought with them their dedication to personal discipline and progressive social ideals. Pictured below is their second building, the "Red Brick Church" located on the corners of Lawrence and Pearl (now Oneida) Streets. It was dedicated in 1888 and remained the congregation's home until 1968. In the late 19th century, First Congregational established two satellite chapels in the Fourth and Fifth Wards, led the temperance battle, and installed Appleton's first film projector. (Images courtesy of the Appleton Public Library; caption provided by John McFadden.)

Congregational Church, Appleton, Wis.

Grace Episcopal Church and Guild Hall was located on the corner Appleton and Edwards (now Washington) Streets. The church building was completed in 1864. The first services were held in 1855. (Image courtesy of the Ken Weiland family.)

St. Paul's Lutheran Church was first known as the German Evangelical Association. It was located at the corner of Morrison and Fisk (now Franklin) Streets. The church was first organized in August 1867. Walter Koester and Irene Steidl were married at the new church July 19, 1919. They are pictured below on the front steps of the church. The German stained glass is visible behind them. (Below image courtesy of the Walter and Irene Koester family.)

Temple Zion, located at 320 North Durkee Street, was organized in 1879 by David Hammel, Jacob Hammel, M. Lyons, S. Marshall, G. Ullman, D.L. Ulman, and Fred Loeb. The temple's first Rabbi was Mayer Sámuel Weisz. Rabbi Weisz was the father of Erich Weisz, better known as Houdini, the famous escape artist.

The Moses Montefiore Temple was located at the corner of Bateman and East Atlantic Streets. It was completed in 1922 and dedicated on June 10, 1923. Mr. Goldin was president of the second synagogue at the time of the dedication. The pioneers began the synagogue in 1890. All the original records are in Yiddish. The name *Moses Montefiore* comes from the distinguished communities in Italy and England. (Image and caption courtesy of Moses Montifiore.)

The exterior of First English Lutheran is pictured above. The cornerstone was laid on October 18, 1931. The building was dedicated on May 22, 1932. Below, the church is decorated for a candlelight service in the 1950s. The two large trees are adorned with Christmas ball ornaments and tinsel. The choir, along with Reverend Rueter, led the congregation in song as they exited the church. (Above image courtesy of the Appleton Public Library; below image courtesy of Gerhard and Lorrain Vogt family.)

The First English Luther League hosted stage plays in the lower level of the church in Fellowship Hall. In April 1939, Clarence Richter directed the play *Ding, Dong, Dumb Bell*. The cast included, from left to right, (first row) Ed Gauerke and Harry Junge; (second row) Bob Maves, Don Ballard, Eunice Reyfeldt, and Marion Maves; (third row) Don Newton, Ralph Junge, Lorrain Junge, and Caroline Staedt; (fourth row) Bill Block, Cliff Hutchinson, Ruth Gust, Leland Brockman, Martin Gauerke, Arelene Ballard, and Helen Aykens. (Image courtesy of Walter and Mickey Schmidt.)

This First English confirmation photograph was taken May 22, 1966. Member Everett Rhode was always willing to take beautiful photographs of this church and its congregation. The students captured here are, from left to right, (first row) Bob Sneen, Jeff Doerschner, Gail Meyer, Judy Kapitzke, Bonnie Koentopp, Joanne Zehren, Christine Sanders, and Connie Zehren; (second row) Lee Streow, Scott Miles, Kenneth Havel, Steven Erbach, Karen Able, Paula Gilbertson, Michelle Piette, Deborah Theis, and Kristine Peters; (third row) John Woehler, Thomas Havel, Jeff Day, Dennis Draphal, Chris Braun, Cindy Burghardt, Lavonne Berkvam, and Peggy Beyer; (fourth row) Larry Crober, Bob Lemke, Roger Froehlich, Kay Schmidt, Ann Beyer, Jacquie Beckmann, Debbie DeBruin, and Judy Haefer; (fifth row) Greg Buss, Catherine Cate, Anne Sosinski, Constance Wieckert, Shirley Kiefer, Judith Bartell, Susan Johnson, and Steven Hilderman; (sixth row) Jeff Wheeler, Steve Fischer, Claire Meyer, Melanie Meyer, Susan Kuzenski, Theodore Meyer, Craig Block, Jeffrey Lautenschlager, and Peter Kliefoth. Pastor Leonard A. Ziemer is on the right, and intern pastor William Metter is on the left. (Image and caption courtesy of Kay Forton.)

The first Zion Evangelical Lutheran Church was a wood-frame building on the corner of Winnebago and Oneida Streets. At the time, the location was on the outskirts of the city. The building was dedicated on May 25, 1884, with some visitors arriving by train to celebrate. All services were conducted in German until 1909. Zion's first school is seen on the left in this c. 1889 image, and the first pastor's residence is visible behind the church. (Image and caption courtesy of Bob Kohl.)

There was no organ inside the first wood-frame building for Zion Evangelical Lutheran Church on the corner of Winnebago and Oneida Streets. The services were accompanied by a brass quintet of local musicians. This photograph, taken around 1899, likely shows the Easter decorations. Mirroring society of the period, women and children were not considered equal to men and were served communion separately. (Image and caption courtesy of Bob Kohl.)

In 1902, the Gothic brick-and-stone Zion Evangelical Lutheran Church was built on the corner of Winnebago and Oneida Streets where Zion's former wood-frame church had been. With the tallest steeple in the city, it is one of the most visible landmarks in Appleton. The three massive bells in the tower were the gift of the children of the church—paid for with weekly collections of their pennies and nickels. The house to the left is the minister's residence. This photograph dates to around 1902 (Image and caption courtesy of Bob Kohl.)

The congregation of St. Matthew Lutheran began worship on the corner of Mason and Lawrence Streets in a modest wooden chapel in 1914. The chapel was replaced with the present structure in 1924, and in 1956, a bell tower was erected adjacent to the church. The three bells were cast in the Netherlands, with the 1,500-pound bell playing the note G, the 800-pound bell, B, and the 440-pound bell, D. (Image and caption courtesy of Allan Wrobel.)

First Baptist Church was located on the Southwest corner of Appleton and Fisk (Franklin) Streets. The church was organized in 1852 by a pastor from Neenah. B.B. Murch, William Remington, and D.H. Bowen were founding members. In 1855, Rev. A Hamilton arrived. The church was completed in 1860.

St. Mary's Catholic Church was formed in 1868 upon the division of the original Catholics of Appleton into two congregations. T. O'Keefe designed the brick structure to seat 1,000 persons. The church is located on State and Seventh Streets. At the time it was built, each side of the front of the building had a 148-foot spire.

Monte Alverno was built in 1934 as a Catholic retreat center. It was erected on land donated to the Capuchins by Kay Merkel. The land included 825 feet of beautiful Fox River waterfront. The building is stone construction and includes a 1964 additional wing and front entry. Above, it was originally built with stone brought by horse and wagon to the location. The building included a chapel with artisan stained-glass windows. The round stained-glass window in the chapel was crafted by Conrad Schmidt Studios. Below is the building before the 1964 addition. (Above image courtesy of the Capuchins Monte Alverno; below image courtesy of John Marx.)

MONTE ALVERNO RETREAT HOUSE, APPLETON, WIS.

St. Joseph's Church was organized in 1868 when it separated from St. Mary's. The Reverend Watkins was the priest at the time. Bishop Hennie of Milwaukee decided that the church should split off from St. Mary's, so St. Mary's became the Irish Catholic congregation, and St. Joseph's, the German Catholic. On November 5, 1869, the new St. Joseph's Church was ready for Mass. Below is an interior view of St. Joseph's Church. (Images courtesy of Jim Krueger.)

Five

BUSINESSES
BIG AND SMALL

This c. 1870 photograph shows the Benoit and Montgomery Drug Store. The store was built in 1855 and served as the offices for several insurance agencies. The store and offices were located on College and Oneida Streets. (Image courtesy of the Appleton Public Library.)

The Odd Fellows Block is located at College Avenue and Morrison Street. The Odd Fellows were formed in 1850. The charter members of the lodge included Wm. Mckracken, Theo. Conkey, N.E. Bailey, Ira W. Bowen, T.S. Buck, and S.B. Beach. (Image courtesy of the Appleton Public Library.)

This business at 718 North Clark Street was owned by Allen A. and Carrie Fraser. A.A. Fraser grew up on a farm in Grand Chute and became a carpenter, eventually opening his own enterprise. His sister Nellie Fraser is standing in the doorway. (Image courtesy of John Marx.)

Charles and Joanna Lindley owned the steam laundry at 707 College Avenue. On the right side, Martin P. VanRyzin Pattern and Model Works is visible. The pattern and model works was located at 586 Durkee Street (now 100 South Durkee Street). On the left, Heckert Shoe Company signage is in place. The photograph was taken in 1908. In the foreground are trolley tracks and the bricks of College Avenue. (Image courtesy of the Ken Weiland family.)

Horse-drawn wagons bring wood and other items to market behind Montgomery's Drug Store on Market Street (now Soldier's Square). Market Street ran from Oneida Street to Morrison Street. The wood was carried by both horse-drawn wagons and sleds. Here, they would barter, trade, sell, and buy commodities of the day. The upstairs of the drugstore included the Wecker newspaper office and a German insurance agency. The sign to the right in the photograph explains that wines and liquors are sold by the pint, quart, and gallon. (Image courtesy of the Ken Weiland family.)

This view looks west at the 600 block of West College Avenue and State Street in 1925. The four-story building on College Avenue between Richmond and Locust Streets was known as the Willy Flour Mill. Samuel R. Willy was a successful businessman, having run the Flour Mills for over 60 years. He served as mayor of Appleton in 1873 and 1874. At the time he became mayor, Appleton had a population of about 7,000 souls, and a total of 20 mills and factories were in operation on the river. In the foreground is a four-story brick building belonging to Marshall Brothers Paper. Samuel, Louis, and Harry Marshall were partners at 618 Richmond Street. (Image courtesy of Michael Broeren.)

William Steidl opened the City Tailor Shop located at 650 Appleton Street (three storefronts from the northeast corner of Appleton and Washington Streets). He worked with local hotels to provide a tailoring and pressing services. He went on to be part owner in both the Brighton Beach and Waverly Beach resorts in their heydays. (Image courtesy of the Steidl family.)

Henry Hauert, proprietor of Hauert Flour, Feed, and Seed, drives the feed truck. The business was located at 645-649 Appleton Street, the northwest corner of Appleton and Washington Streets. (Image courtesy of Gretchen Hauert.)

Fox River Chevrolet received the delivery of all the new Chevrolets for Appleton and the surrounding communities. They lined them on 400 block of west College Avenue for a promotion. The block also included Walker Drugs, the L.R. Doll Restaurant, and Kasten Brothers Quality Shoes. This block is now the location of Appleton Performing Arts Center. (Image courtesy of Jim Krueger.)

Peter Christensen is pictured in the Tschank and Christensen truck. The family business was started in 1921 at 652 Richmond Street and continues today. (Image courtesy of the Christensen family.)

The John Leithen Shoe Repair Shop was located at 616 West College Avenue. A view inside of the shop shows the shoes, repair stations, and tools for leather. John and Fred Leithen are working on shoes. (Image courtesy of Rosemarie DeBruin.)

The Appleton Wire Works was located on the northeast corner of Atlantic and Union Streets. In 1896, Albert Weissenborn joined his brother-in-law William Buchanan, his close friend and nephew Gus Buchanan, and John Buchanan in founding the Appleton Wire Works. By 1910, it had grown to be the second-largest wire-weaving plant in the country, and the largest in the West. In 1912, the business was refinanced into a partnership between Albert and his nephew Gus. Albert Weissenborn served as president of the company from 1912 until his death in 1938. (Image courtesy of Dave Buss.)

Engelbert and Anna Liethen bought some dusty buildings on the northwest corner of College Avenue and Richmond Street in 1916 to start a grain and feed mill business. They ran the grain mill with their five sons and two daughters. In 1929, they sold the location and purchased the pictured site at the northwest corner of College and Badger Avenues. Here, they erected a five-story concrete and metal building. Mules Maude and Jenny made up the team that Bob Leithen drove to deliver feed. (Image courtesy of Carol McIntyre.)

Standard Oil Company was located at 301-305 East College Avenue (the pre-1925 address was 711 East College Avenue). A.W. Miller was the agent. The company had other filling stations on West College Avenue and North Oneida Street. (Image courtesy of the Ken Weiland family.)

St. Elizabeth Hospital started as an 11-room, 2-story frame house located at 110 East Fremont Street. The Franciscan Sisters' first patients came in by horse-drawn wagon. Tom Nooyen was the hospital's first surgical patient. In 1900, the hospital secured an eight-acre donation and built a two-story brick facility on the property. In 1920, the hospital was increased to 55 beds. (Image courtesy of the Appleton Public Library.)

Construction of Home Mutual's new corporate office at 2401 South Memorial Drive was completed in 1963 under the leadership of Gordon Bubolz (pictured), son of company founder Julius Bubolz. The mutual insurance company originated in 1900 at Julius's farmhouse near Seymour, Wisconsin, and later moved to Appleton. In 1986, Home Mutual was renamed Secura Insurance. Today, it partners with independent agents across 12 states to provide insurance for businesses, homes and cars, farms, agribusiness, nonprofits, and special events. (Image courtesy of SECURA Insurance; caption provided by Steve Smits.)

Walter Sigl surveys his Sigl Bros. men's clothing store in 1947. Walter and Robert Sigl operated the business at 322 West College Avenue from about 1929 until 1954. (Image courtesy of the Joan V. Hurley family.)

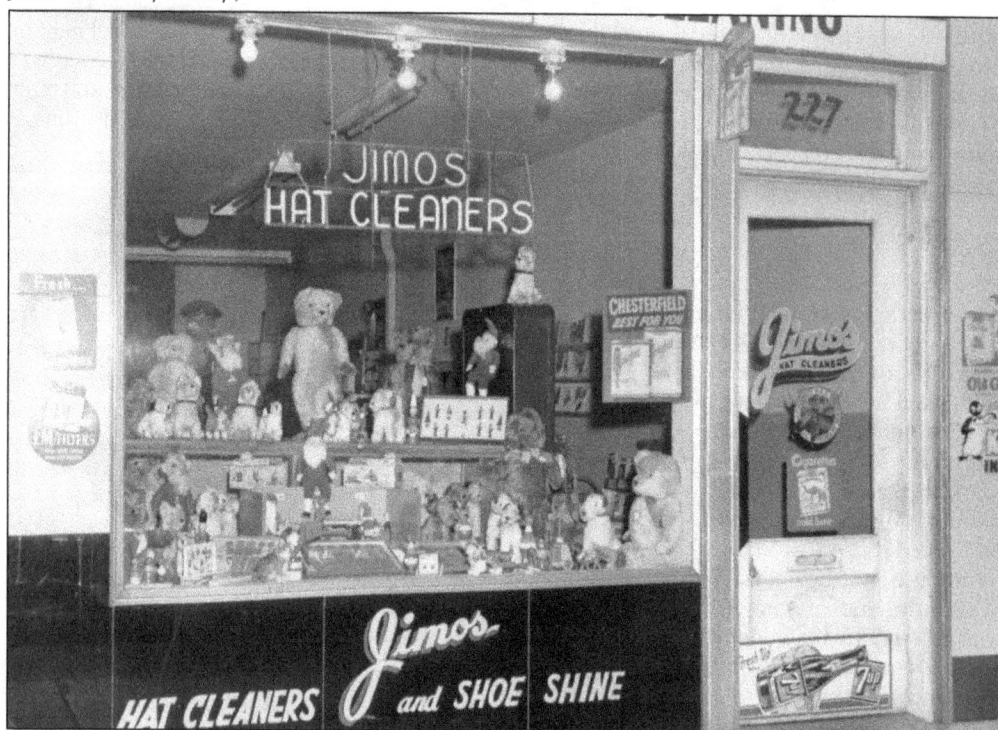

According to Irene Gamsky, Andrew Jimos came to America at the age of 16, a Greek immigrant. Within 10 years, he had learned English, become a citizen of the United States, bought the building at 203/205 College Avenue, and married 18-year-old Georgia Andropolis. They made their home at 611 East Pacific Street. He contributed to the community as an Outagamie County Board supervisor and Appleton water commissioner. Both Andrew and Georgia Jimos were among the founders of St. Nicholas Greek Orthodox Church. Jimos's hat cleaners and shoe-shining shop's last location was 227 East College Avenue, pictured here. (Image courtesy of Jim Krueger.)

Gloudemans Department Store, seen in these interior and exterior views, was located in downtown Appleton. The people posed in the interior include, from left to right, Lee Fischer, Gwen Dittmer, Adelaide Kuberg, Agnes Stein, Loretta Greisbach, Louise Kuether, and Leone Coonen. (Images courtesy of Joan Giuliani.)

Heid Music was located at 215 East College but, in 1957, moved to 308 East College Avenue. Peter Heid established the business in 1948 and was joined by partner Buck Jensen. (Images and caption courtesy of Paul Heid.)

Clarence Hinzman started Appleton Bicycle Shop on Soldier's Square December 5, 1939. In 1950, he moved the shop to 121 South State Street. The interior and exterior of the shop are pictured here. The shop sold Schwinn bicycles, accessories, and lawn mowers, and also sharpened ice skates. The interior photograph shows a clock on the wall that still hangs today. The 1961 exterior sign had neon tubes running over the letters. Paul Hinzman took over from his father and continues on today with his daughter Gwen and son-in-law Joe Sargeant. (Images courtesy of Paul Hinzman.)

Seven years after arriving in Appleton from Germany, trained masons Fred and Herman Hoffmann founded the Hoffmann Construction Company in 1888. Shown is the construction of the First Congregational Church (1888) at the corner of Oneida and Lawrence Streets. Other notable buildings constructed by the company include Columbus Elementary School (1892), Zion Lutheran Church (1903), Wilson Junior High School (1931), Outagamie Courthouse (1940), St. Therese Church (1953), and Valley Fair Mall (1953). In the 1950s, the family and company dropped the second *n* from their name. (Images courtesy of Hoffman Construction; caption provided by Christine Williams.)

The Conway Hotel started out in the 1880s as the Outagamie House, later becoming known as Sherman Hotel, and then, the Conway. There were three generations of the Conway family involved with the hotel over its more-than-80-year history. The business saw many changes over time, and it was one of the first hotels in the state to have electricity, steam heat, and many other amenities. The Conway was seen by many as one of the top-notch hotels of its time. It hosted many travelers, including Richard Nixon as he made his bid for the 1968 presidential election. (Image courtesy of Jim Krueger; caption provided by Gary Schierl.)

Appleton State Bank opened in 1911 at 851 College Avenue (now 221-223 West College Avenue). In 1931, they doubled the size of the facilities and had one of the most modern vaults in the state. In 1953, Gus Zuehlke, president, started plans to extend the size of the bank. Property was acquired on College Avenue, and in 1962, demolition and reconstruction began. The bank was built in two sections. The west half was completed first, while the old bank continued to operate. Then, the east half was completed. (Image courtesy of BMO Harris Bank, Douglas Paschen.)

August Winter & Sons and Oscar J. Boldt Construction Co. signs hang on the construction at College Avenue and Superior Street. Work is being done on the concrete of the building's top floor with a crane. In the rear of the photograph, Gibson Chevrolet is visible on the corner of Lawrence and Superior Streets. (Image courtesy of BMO Harris Bank, Douglas Paschen.)

The southeast corner of College Avenue and Superior Street included, from left to right, the Appleton State Bank, the Home Appliance Company, Jimos Hat Cleaners, and the Firestone tire dealer, seen here in the 1950s. (Image courtesy of BMO Harris Bank, Douglas Paschen.)

The Aid Association for Lutherans building was located on the northeast corner of College Avenue and Superior Street in 1964. This photograph shows the crane working on the 10-story addition. Walgreens is also visible on the right. (Image courtesy of Dave Buss.)

Above is a beautiful view of East College Avenue from Oneida Street. In the distance is the Lawrence University chapel. Below is a beautiful view of West College Avenue from Oneida Street, taken around 1930. (Images courtesy of the Ken Weiland family.)

Six

EATING, DRINKING, AND BEING MERRY

C.R. Nagreen's candy and ice-cream shop was at 317 East College Avenue in downtown Appleton for decades. This photograph, taken around 1900, shows Charles Nagreen on the right. Charles is probably better known as Seymour's "Hamburger Charlie" since he is credited with inventing the hamburger at the 1885 Outagamie County Fair in Seymour. According to his niece Sophia Nagreen (who celebrated her 101st birthday in 2014), he was also the first person to put ice cream on a stick. (Image and caption courtesy of Bob Kohl.)

Charles Reitzner was the proprietor of the Union House at 1005 College Avenue (the southwest corner of College Avenue and State Street). The Union House had boarding upstairs and a sample room below. Reitzner served both wines and liquors. These gentlemen are standing on the wooden, raised sidewalk in front, and a lady peeks out from a window on the left. In the distance, a trolley is traveling down State Street. (Image courtesy of the Tom Butler family.)

Appleton Brewing and Malting Company started at 701 Lake Street. Frank Fries was the owner and manager from 1899 to 1917. Edward C. Schmidt also bottled beer at 701 Lake Street from 1899 until 1917. The truck pictured here is loaded for delivery of the barrels of beer. (Image courtesy of the History Museum at the Castle.)

William J. and Marie Eggert's hotel was located at 301-303 North Appleton Street. The Eggert Hotel also included a sample room and dining hall. Above, men gather in the bar for a drink, and advertisements for Rolling Fork Bourbon adorn the wall in about 1917. The spittoons are visible on the wood floor of the bar. Below, about 15 men fill the dining hall for meals cooked by Marie Eggert (standing beside Bill at the back of the photograph). The image shows a small buffet table and a bell to be rung for additional service. (Image courtesy of Dave and Barb Daelke.)

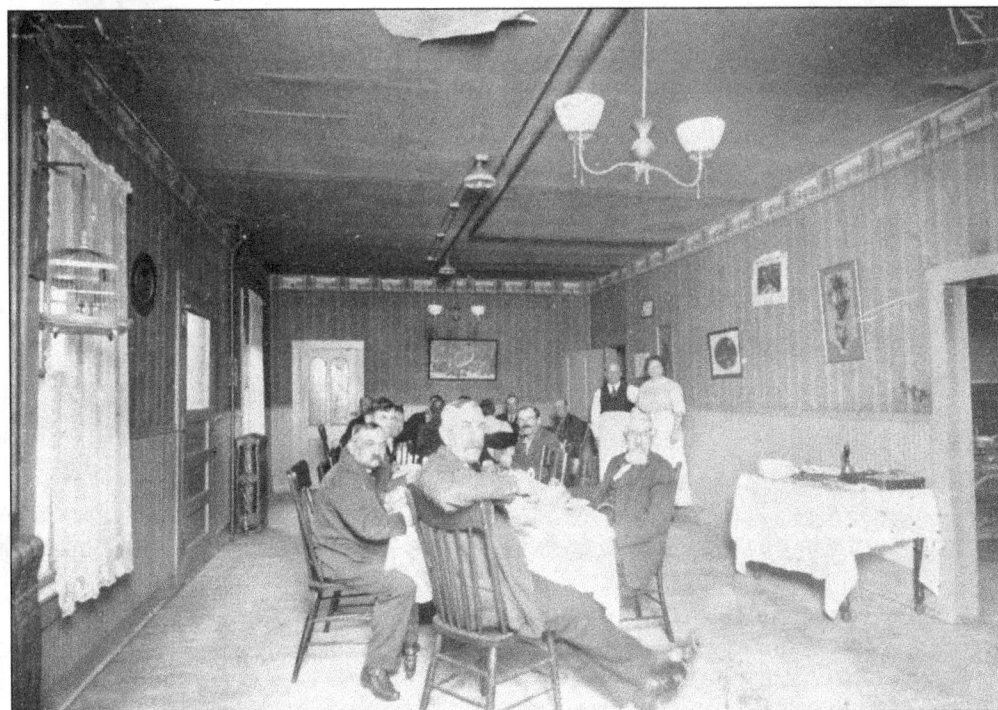

John and Kate Hollenbach are pictured here standing in their grocery store at 513 Appleton Street. The calendar on the wall is turned to April 1926. In 1925, there were 54 small, individual grocers in the city of Appleton. (Image courtesy of Rosemarie DeBruin.)

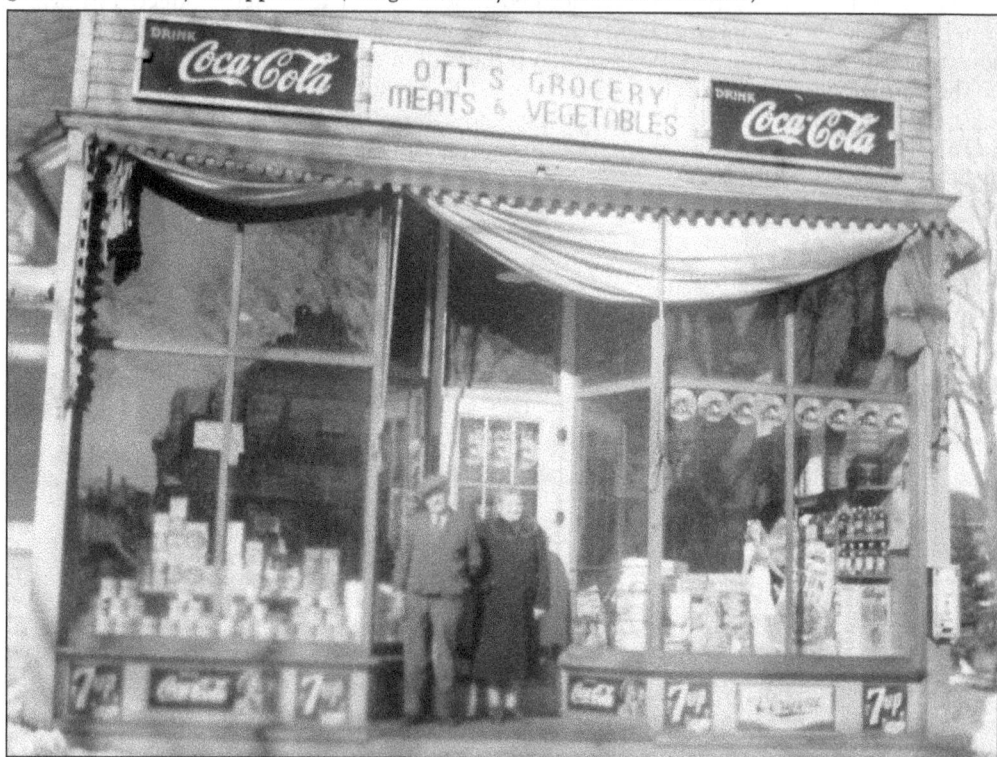

Ott's Grocery was located at 1006 East North Street. Paul and Anna Ott are standing in front of their store in 1945. In those years, Coca-Cola was a big sponsor of signage for businesses, and many Appleton enterprises in this era had Coca-Cola signs. The advertisements in the right side of the front window include oversized boxes of Kellogg's cereal. (Image courtesy of John Marx.)

A.J. Shannon was a wholesale grocer located at 598-600 College Avenue (northwest corner of College Avenue and Union Street). They stocked choice vegetables and other pantry items. The photograph shows baskets and bushels of potatoes, squash, and more overflowing with a fall harvest. (Image courtesy of Mark Moderson.)

The Thrifty Superette Grocery was located at 1109 West Wisconsin Avenue. George Schirmacher was partner and manager. (Image courtesy of the History Museum at the Castle.)

The Giebisch family had a meat market at 975 College Avenue (now 530 West College Avenue). They are pictured standing on a wooden sidewalk outside of the front of the store. Family members include Anton and Hattie and children Milton, Alice, and Herbert. (Image courtesy of Karen Van Lyssal.)

The F. Stoffel & Son Market was located at 839 West College Avenue (now the 400 block) in about 1910. Fred and his daughter Katherine are pictured. Fred Stoffel passed away in the mid-1930s. He had four children: Marie, who was married and expecting a child when she passed away in the 1917–1918 flu epidemic; Elizabeth, who married Ervin Heyman and lived in Green Bay; Katherine, who married John Liethen, with whom she owned a secondhand and antique shop at 612 West College Avenue for 25 years; and Joseph, who married Ada Carley and later moved from Appleton. Fred Stoffel's house still stands at the corner of 226 South State Street. (Image courtesy of Rosemarie DeBruin.)

Brothers John and Leonard Jacobs purchased the Wentink-Steidl meat market in 1945. The Jacobs family carries on the tradition of German recipes and fresh-cut meats to this day. The store has seen a few remodels, but according to the owners Ed and his son Luke Jacobs, it still has the same "old" feel. They run the smokehouse with real wood chips all week long. (Image courtesy of the Jacobs family.)

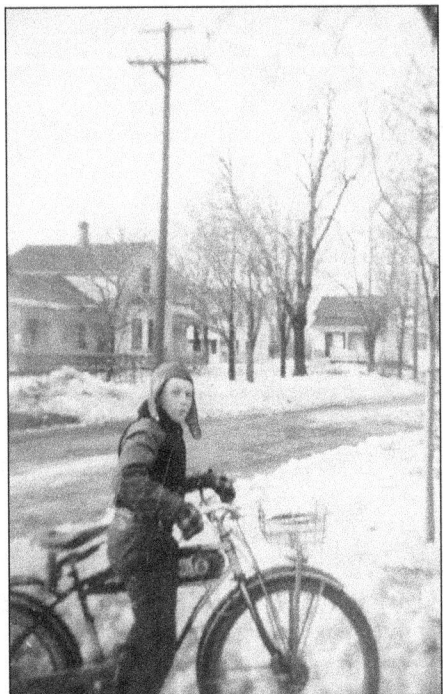

The Wentink Meat Market was opened in 1892 by Theodore Wentink on the corner of Pacific and Lawe Streets. Wentink's daughter Mary Ann married George Steidl in 1901, thus beginning the Wentink-Steidl years. George and Mary Ann carried on in the family business, employing relatives. Here, Junior Koester, nephew of George, has finished delivering meat on his bicycle and is arriving home in the Fourth Ward. It was uphill both ways from the meat market to the Fourth Ward. (Image courtesy of the Steidl family.)

J.B. Weiland drives the team carrying the Tellulah Springs Water. Tellulah Springs, initially known as Harriman's Springs, was a sulfur spring located on land originally belonging to J.E. Harriman. Its eventual name, *Tellulah*, is a Native American word meaning, "running water." (Image courtesy of the Ken Weiland family.)

Henry John Koester, a German immigrant, began his business as a hand-bottled and horse-and-wagon–delivered beverage company in 1912. Here, H.J. Koester is ready to drive the team while his wife, Helene Schwahn Koester, and daughter Isabelle Koester check the bottles. (Image courtesy of the Koester family.)

Above, Henry Koester stands between his grandson Junior (left) and son Walter (right) inside the bottling plant. By the 1930s, an advertisement declared Koester's Beverages "a modern plant with efficient sterilizing and bottling machinery." A delivery truck also was now part of the business. Koester's delivered soda pop to many homes, taverns, fairs, and church picnics. Customers could also stop and select their soda, placing it into a metal six-pack carrier or wooden case of 24. In the summer, people would sit down in Helene Koester's garden with a nice, ice-cold soda. Many family members worked at the "pop shop" for their first job or joined the crew to bottle a large order. (Images courtesy of the Koester family; caption provided by Kay Forton.)

Templin's Beer Depot was located on North Mason Street. Red and Clay Templin, brothers and owners, are standing behind the counter. They bought McGilligan's after the war and ran the beer depot for 50 years. (Image and caption courtesy of Jim Krueger.)

After a long day working to set up the new St. Joseph's School, Fr. Alphonse Heckler and parishioners partake of some beer from George Walter Brewing. (Image courtesy of Jim Krueger.)

George Steidl's family celebrated his 75th birthday with a party in the ballroom of the Hotel Appleton. The guests included his wife, Minnie; his brothers and sisters-in-law Joe and Aura, Bill and Dell, Chris and Martha, Herb and Anna, and Frank and Jennie; and sisters and brothers-in-law Augusta and Theo Sanders, and Irene and Walter Koester. His children included sons Lawrence and Clem and daughters Theodora and Leona. There were also many nieces and nephews in attendance. (Image courtesy of Kay Forton.)

Appleton's Lady Eagles celebrated their 20-year anniversary on April 28, 1948. The charter members from 1928 included, from left to right, (first row) Kate Deml, Theresa Schiltz, Ida Brandt, Mrs. Koll, Lilly Albrecht, Hazel Popp Koester, Helen Schwahn Koester, and May Strutz; (second row) Agnes Hofenbecker, Zada Gosha, Sada Fisk, Kate Hoffman, Margaret Grearson, and Mrs. Knaack; (third row) Meta Hintz, Mrs. Boldt, Lottie Austin, Gladys Koerner, Helen Gregorious, Mrs. Hoh, Mrs. Weber, and Mrs. Desten. Absent were Mrs. Dick and Mrs. Rademacher. (Image courtesy of the Helene Schwahn Koester family.)

The residence of J.E. and Cecilia Harriman was located at Bellaire Park, overlooking the Fox River. The home had stunning windows and architecture. J.E. Harriman studied at Lawrence University and practiced law with Messrs. Jewett and Hudd of Appleton. He was elected mayor of Appleton in April 1876. (Image courtesy of Mark Moderson.)

Nathanial M. Edwards was a civil engineer of the old Green Bay and Mississippi Canal Company. His home was located at 699 Lawrence Street (now 316 East Lawrence Street). (Image courtesy of Mark Moderson.)

Seven

WHERE THEY LIVED AND PLAYED

The boys of the south side enjoyed the Tellulah Park area. Here, a party of hunters shows off their spoils at camp. The camp included a shack called the Tellulah Clubhouse. The first two men on the left are Hank Noffke and Bill Noffke, respectively. Other members of the club included Shorty Smith, Otto Sternough, and Sy Young. (Image and caption courtesy of Raymond Noffke.)

The first apartments in Appleton were owned by Reeder Smith. They were located on Lawrence Street overlooking the Mill Creek Ravine (now the east side of Jones Park). The apartments were home to many Appleton residents, including superintendent of schools Carrie Morgan. (Image courtesy of the Appleton Public Library.)

Col. Henry Levake Blood was the proprietor of the of the Levake House at Morrison Street and College Avenue. The Levake House was a popular stop for weary travelers in the 1870s. John F. Johnston took over the property not long before it was destroyed by fire in 1872. (Image courtesy of the Appleton Public Library.)

The Erb Park land was purchased in 1923 from Herman Erb, a mayor of Appleton. The park was eventually developed in 1940. It included a new pool, known as the "bird bath" for its shape. Seen here is Erb Park's entrance after a winter storm in 1940. The park's many trees are covered in ice and snow, creating a winter wonderland. (Image courtesy of Bob Kohl.)

Jones Park, the second park dedicated in Appleton, was donated in 1909 by George Jones. Originally, it encompassed the area from the corner of Prospect and Oneida Streets north to Atlantic Street. Its north end became known as "Packard Hill" and is now known as Arbutus Park. Here, families skate on the ice in Jones Park below Lawrence Street in about 1930. Skating at the Jones Park ice rink continues to be a part of Appleton's winters. (Image courtesy of Bob Kohl.)

Bellaire Park is known today as Peabody Park. *Bellaire* comes from the French for "fine air." The bridge in the background is Pacific Street. Often, ravine parks started out as citizens' garbage-dumping sites, and children of the 1920s and 1930s fondly remember finding "treasures in the ravines." (Image courtesy of Dave Kalz.)

Linwood Driving Park was a place to see the races in their many different forms, from horses to bicycles. The park offered a large grandstand for dynamic views of the action. Appleton even hosted the 1896 state bicycling meet. This picture shows horse and cart racing. The park was located on the northwest corner of College Avenue and Linwood Street. (Image courtesy of Michael Broeren.)

The Appleton Boat Club (later known as the Appleton Yacht Club), according to historian Sue Palermo, began in 1921. Members purchased an old boat factory from the city, and one of their first projects moved the building closer to the water. In 1932, six men filed incorporation papers with the State of Wisconsin to officially begin the Appleton Yacht Club. The purpose: "to promote and foster the spirit of boating, to guard and protect the interests of members who are owners of power boats, to inculcate among its members a knowledge of the rules of navigation and naval courtesy, to encourage and conduct races, cruises, club runs, water carnivals, and aquatic events for the entertainment of the citizens of Appleton and to encourage harmony and good fellowship among its members in every way possible." (Image courtesy of Mary Schulz.)

Frank Steidl ran a boat on the Fox River from Appleton to Neenah-Menasha out to Lake Winnebago. The men are pictured here at Lehman's Landing Appleton. The picture captures early spring as there is still snow on the riverbank in the background. (Image courtesy of the Steidl family.)

Through rain, snow, sleet, or sun, people shopped on College Avenue. Here, a young lady peeks out from behind a snow pile on East College Avenue on March 28, 1931. The stores had signs that lit up; the bulbs in the Thiede and Palace signs are visible at left. The Odd Fellows building stands on the right at the corner of College Avenue and Morrison Street. (Image courtesy of Kay Forton.)

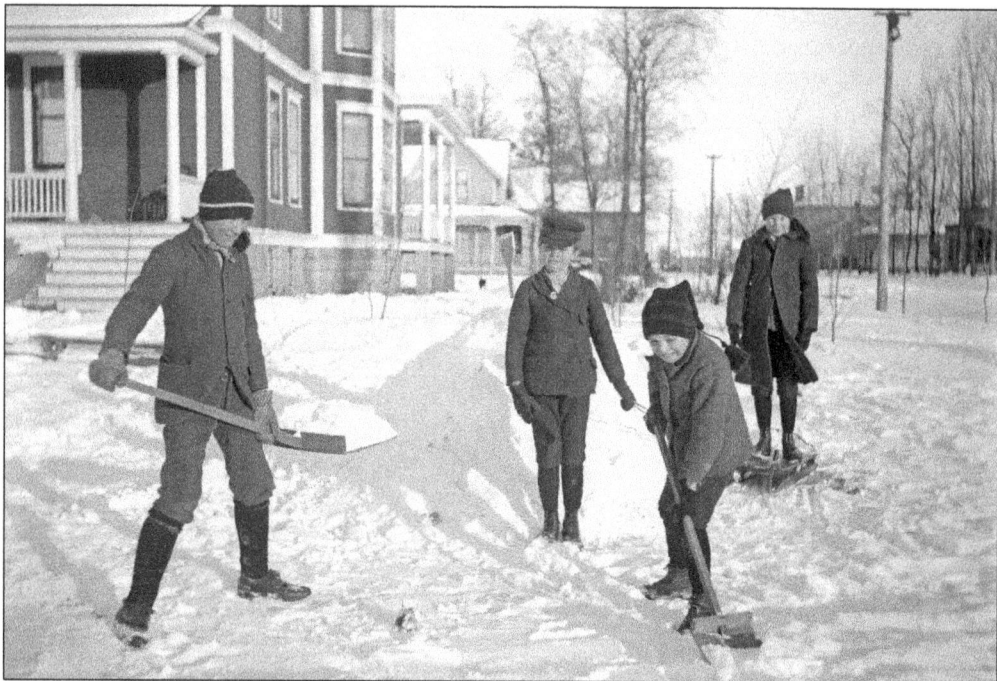

The Galpin boys shovel snow at 983 North Superior Street (now 1203) in about 1900. A young boy in the back stands on top of a sled. The joy and sheer delight is clear in their faces, and they are all wearing warm wool mittens and hats. Their father, Algernon, was proprietor of Galpin and Son's Hardware. (Image courtesy of Jon Porter.)

Sisters Helen (left) and Caroline (right) Koester walk to downtown Appleton from the Fourth Ward in about 1936. The downtown was a popular destination for the library, movies, shopping, and eating. The Rio Theatre graces the background of the photograph. (Image courtesy of the Helen Koester Schmidt and Caroline Koester Staedt families.)

The Rio opened in November 1929 as the Fox Theatre. Its name changed to Rio in the 1930s, and it remained in operation until 1959. The theater held 2,000 seats, and a Wurlitzer organ was installed in it in 1929. (Image courtesy of Dave Kalz.)

In this 1940 view, young people line up at the police department. The police department hosted many events to teach bicycle safety, and if one got in trouble on his or her bike, bike court was held on Saturday mornings with Officer Radtke. (Image courtesy of Arne Nettekoven.)

People line College Avenue for the Soap Box Derby sponsored by the Jaycees. The first derby took place in 1962, with 18 boys signing up to join in the fun on July 15. Here, two soapbox cars race down from the platform located east of Division Street and College Avenue. The Viking Theatre advertises an Elvis Presley picture, and the large neon Aid Association for Lutherans sign rises in the background. (Image courtesy of the Appleton Public Library.)

Rose M. Caitlin, the daughter of George and Rose H. Caitlin, grew up in the bridge tender's house. Here, she is posed with her dog, the railroad swing bridge behind her. The Cherry Street bridge, built in 1922, is visible in the background. The bridge was renamed the Soldier's and Sailor's Memorial Bridge in 1928 (now the Memorial Drive Bridge). (Image courtesy of Mary Schulz.)

Pictured is the upper lock at Appleton. This photograph, taken in 1912 by J.E. Stimson, shows two barges and a small boat waiting as the lock tender turns the wheel to open up the large floodgates. (Image courtesy of Mark Moderson.)

The Valley Fair Mall opened in 1955. In this c. 1950s photograph taken outside of the mall, the judge is making notes for a dog show. (Image courtesy of Hoffman Corporation.)

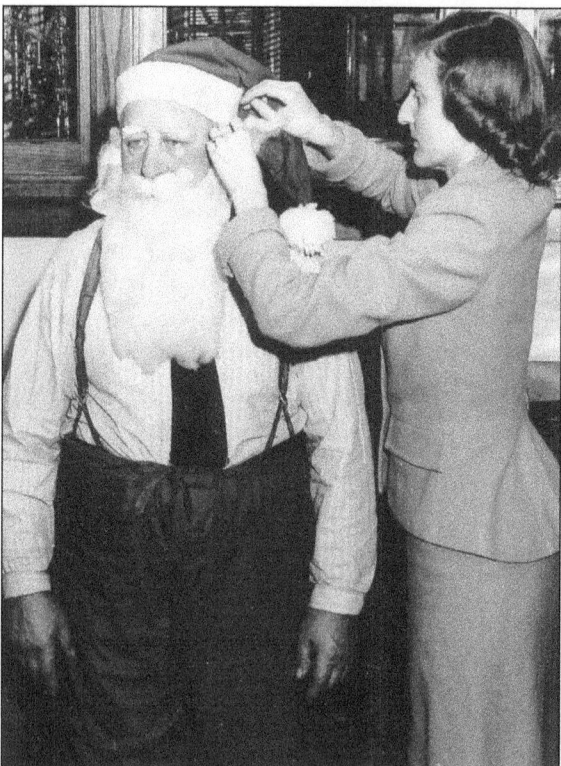

Bill Eggert, superintendent of buildings and grounds for the Appleton Public Schools, gets ready to play Santa. Bill's secretary helps him with the finishing touches before he goes out from school to school to surprise and delight the children. (Image courtesy of Dave and Barb Daelke.)

The Koester's Pop bowling team was called the Orange Squeeze. A clever news headline from the *Appleton Post Crescent* in 1926 said, "Orange Squeeze Pin Artists Trim Oshkosh." The team, which included E. Dunn, V. Wenzlaff, M. Tornow, G. Koerner, and S. Roudenbush, often bowled at the Arcade located at 119 North Appleton Street. (Image courtesy of the Walter and Irene Koester family.)

The Hippodrome Roller Skating Palace was located at 680 College Avenue, pictured here around 1915. Roller skating was very popular. The Steidl brothers, Joe, John, and Bill, were the proprietors. The building was originally the armory in Appleton. (Image courtesy of the Steidl family.)

George and Josephine Klein built their home at 1516 West Franklin Street in 1932. Appleton was expanding west in the 1930s. Many of the homes in this neighborhood have the same style of brick architecture. George was employed by Wisconsin Michigan Power Company, and he also played in the 121st Field Artillery Band and the Appleton City Band. (Image courtesy of Barbara Hirn.)

Henry and Helene (Schwahn) Koester built their home in 1900 at 707 Main Street in the Fourth Ward. In 1925, the entire city of Appleton's address system was changed, and the home is now addressed as 203 South Mckinley Street. When it was built, it had a view of the river valley, and Helene could sit on her front porch and watch Henry returning from deliveries all the way across the river on Lake Street (now Old Oneida Street). Here, Helene sits on the porch steps at left. On the porch, seated, is daughter Isabel. Standing are son Walter (left) and Roy (right). (Image courtesy of the Henry and Helene Koester family.)

Gustav and Lena Reffke are pictured at their home located at 943 Lake Street. Their children, in order of age, were Augusta, Lena, William, Theodore, Hazel, and Helen. The house is a "ghost house," meaning it is no longer standing. The post-1925 address was 1708 South Oneida Street. (Image courtesy of Karen Van Lyssl.)

The Joseph and Carrie (Hagen) Steidl family lived at 1080 Eighth Street in the Old Third Ward. They built their home in 1870. Joseph, a carpenter, built many of the early Appleton buildings. This c. 1898 photograph shows the family in front of and behind the wooden fencing seen in many early Appleton homes. The family members include parents Joe and Carrie; grandmother Anna; daughters Augusta and Irene; and sons George, Chris, William, Frank, and Herbert. In 1925, the house was renumbered 734 West Eighth Street. (Image courtesy of the Joe and Carrie Steidl family.)

Irene (Steidl) Koester hangs laundry in the backyard of her home at 1216 South Monroe Street. The house was built in 1927. In early Appleton, people did their laundry by hand and line dried their clothes. The Sacred Heart School can be seen in the background. (Image courtesy of the Irene Koester family.)

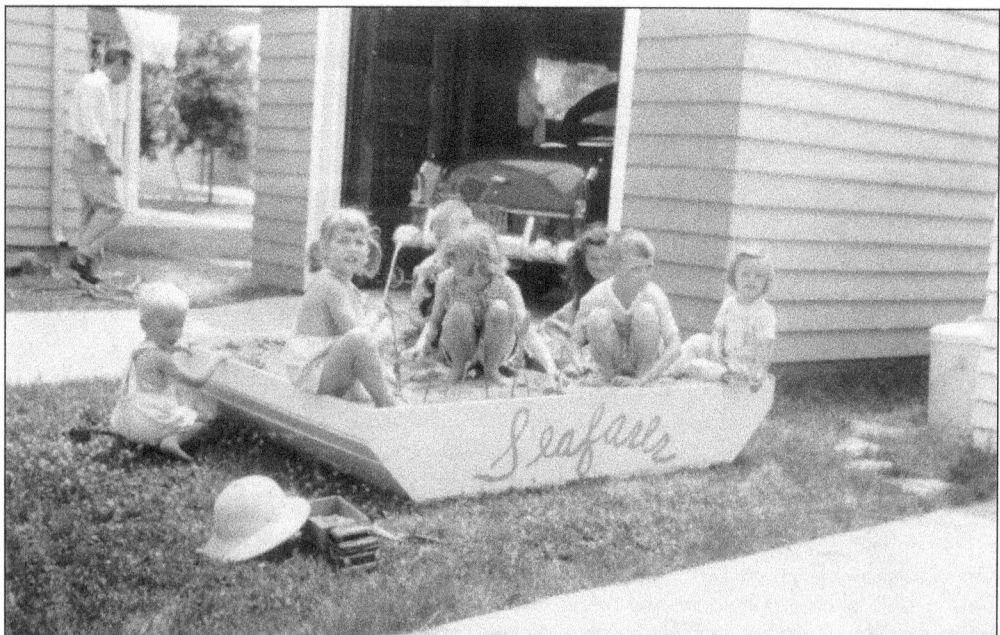

Ken Sager built this sandbox for his children between the Sager and Williamson homes at 525 North Douglas Street. The children pictured here in 1953 include Steve Willaimson, Laura Williamson, Marsha Brewer, and Kris Sager. (Image courtesy of Kris and Ann Sager.)

Here is a westward view of Appleton's College Avenue. The businesses included the First National Bank, John Ross, Enterline Shoes, and Elite Theatre, all visible on the north side of the street. Appletonians would drive to shop and catch a show. The water tower on Walnut Street rises in the background. (Image courtesy of Dave Buss.)

This aerial photograph gives a majestic view of Appleton, from the intersection of College and Badger Avenues in the foreground to the Fox River in the background. The paper mills of Appleton, where many residents went to work each day, crowd the shores of the river and the canals. (Image courtesy of Carol McIntyre.)

95

The railroads provided transportation for both people and goods. The Soo Line Passenger Depot was located on the north side of College Avenue between Bennett and Locust Streets. During the Cuban Missile Crisis, the 32nd Division from Appleton left from this depot to go to Fort Lewis, Washington. (Image and caption courtesy of Dave Kalz.)

Eight

WHERE THEY LEARNED

The Second Ward school was a two-story brick building constructed at a cost of $5,000. The school was known as the Hercules School. Finished in 1859, the brick structure replaced an original wooden one that had burned in 1855. The first high school classes in Appleton were held there in 1859–1860. Ryan's *History of Outagamie County* lists the first graduating class in the 1878. The class consisted of 10 students: Delia Grimes, F.W. Harriman, Margaret McCormick, Emma Mory, J.B. Murphy, Eula Putnam, Flora Randall, George Thompson, Lillie Turner, and W.P. Verity.

The Fifth Ward school was built in 1877 between Bennett, Elsie, Locust, and Lorain Streets. In the 1880s, the curriculum at Appleton schools included arithmetic, geography, practical grammar, botany, zoology, and German. In 1884–1885, the Fifth Ward school had 127 pupils and 3 teachers.

The Third Ward school was located on the northeast corner of Fifth and Locust Streets. It was built in 1884, and the architect was William Waters. The building had a French-style roof and a clock tower with four faces on it. The brick used consisted of contrasting bands of light colors. It was later known as the "Old Jefferson School." The facility was razed in the 1950s and replaced with a new Jefferson building on the corner of Mason Street and Prospect Avenue.

This is the inside of the Third Ward school located at Fifth and Locust Streets. The sixth-grade class includes, from the front of the row to the back, (closest to the board on the left side) Hilda H., Alice S., Tom S., Margaret M., Anna B., Undige S., and Ray P.; (middle row) Walter W., Luella B., Harry P., Sam H., Renfrew K., Russell K., and Lulu S., (foreground right side) Iola E., Eddie W., Mildred M., Neil H., Marie S., Irene S., and Ed S. (Image courtesy of the Irene Steidl Koester family.)

Ryan High School was built by the second district in 1881–1883. Charles Hove was the architect. In a special section to the *Northwestern* in January 1904, the destruction of Ryan High School was detailed: "Ryan High School was burned at four o'clock this morning, being completely destroyed, with a loss of $30,000 and insurance of $25,000. The library, valuable records and much property belonging to teachers and pupils were destroyed. The origin of the fire is unknown, but the blaze is supposed to be due to the heating apparatus, which was old and defective. At the risk of their lives, Professor Smith, teacher of German, Norman Frisbie, a student, and William Zuehlke, member of the board of education, entered the second story by means of ladders set against the swaying walls and saved the valuable 'Miss Ruth Marshall' microscopes from destruction." (Above image courtesy of Michael Broeren; below image courtesy of First Congregational Church.)

The first St. Joseph's School opened in 1868 with the parish. The first building to house the school was erected in 1880. An interior view of St. Joseph's Grade School (above) shows it filled with light. This picture from the 1916–1917 timeframe shows a class of about 60 students working on their reading lessons. An angel statue looks on the from the rear corner of the room. The fourth student from the left in the front row is George Klein. George was born in Appleton 1905 and graduated from eighth grade at St. Joseph's School in 1920. The image below shows the school's exterior before it was razed in 1950. (Above image courtesy of Barbara Hirn; below image courtesy of Jim Krueger.)

Roosevelt Junior High was built in 1925. This photograph shows the graduating class of 1946. Alfred Oosterhous was principal of Roosevelt from its opening in 1925 until his retirement in 1947. Herbert Heble in *Articles of Public Schools* reported that Roosevelt had 19 classrooms, 4 shops for boys, 2 home-arts laboratories, a library, a gymnasium with showers and dressing rooms, and an auditorium. (Image courtesy of Clarice Belling.)

These are members of Roosevelt Junior High School's Boy Scout Troop No. 12 in front of the first-aid tent in 1933 at the "Camp-o-Ral" in Appleton's Pierce Park. The scrapbook information under the photograph names identifies those standing (from left to right) as Schwerbel, Gardner, S.M. Doerfler, and A.S.M. Peterson, and those kneeling as Teasley, Buesing, and Sieth. Ralph Schwerbel went on to be a war correspondent in the Philippines for the *Appleton Post Crescent* during World War II until he was killed in action. (Image and caption courtesy of Bob Kohl.)

Zion Evangelical Lutheran Church had just finished construction of its second school in 1894 when this photograph was taken. A bigger school had to be built to accommodate the growing numbers of students from the population of new German immigrants in Appleton. It stood on Commercial Street just east of Oneida Street until it was torn down in 1928 to make room for Zion to build the school building that stands there today. The carpentry contract for the 1894 school was $2,650. (Image and caption courtesy of Bob Kohl.)

Fourth-grade McKinley School students pose on the front steps in about 1928. Standing on the first step with his arms folded is Ken Schmidt. Little did he know then that he would someday be the superintendent of the buildings and grounds for Appleton Public Schools. (Image courtesy of the Ken Schmidt family.)

The Fourth Ward school later known as McKinley Elementary School was dedicated New Year's Day 1890. These students are the fourth-grade class of 1929. Old McKinley was torn down, and the location is now the site of Jaycee Park in Appleton. (Image courtesy of the Koester family.)

The McKinley Junior High School staff in 1936–1937 included, from left to right (first row) Mr. Monthieth (gym), Miss Nenacheck (office), Miss Shannon (science), Miss Gillman (gym), Mr. Nelson (business science), back row Mr. Ryan (art), Miss Parkensen (English), and Miss Alvord (home economics). (Image courtesy of the Koester family.)

McKinley School provides a backdrop for a group of ninth-grade young ladies and a young fellow peeking over the top from his bicycle. From left to right are (first row), Lois Dupler, Betty Mortenson, Constance Kasper, Virginia Burk, Mildred Lisering, Alice McCanter, and Faliemow Nelson; (second row) Helen Kirk, Betty Nelson, Ruth Seitz, and Norbert Roeland. (Image courtesy of the Koester family.)

Appleton High School was constructed in 1904, marking the union of all of Appleton's previous high schools into one building. Later, the building was rededicated and named for longtime superintendent of schools Carrie Morgan. (Image courtesy of the Tom Butler family.)

Appleton High School students created and wore a "living flag" for the World War I homecoming parade in July 1919, pictured here on the school's lawn. There are 49 stars on the flag. The school took up one city block and was bordered by Harris Street, Oneida Street, North Street, and Morrison Street. (Image courtesy of Laura Leimer.)

The Appleton School Board considered many sites for a new high school, including Badger Avenue and Mason Street, City Park, the Salm property, a State Street site, Riverview Country Club, the Schneider Farm, Pierce Park, and the Spencer Street property. They ultimately chose the site at Badger Avenue and Mason Street. Herbert Helble led the early charge to build a facility to relieve the crowded conditions of Appleton High School. The school was built in 1938 with Herbert Helble its first principal. (Image courtesy of the Tom Butler family.)

The large building in the lower-right corner of the picture is Wilson Junior High, dedicated in 1925. Wilson is bounded by Badger Avenue, Mason Street, and Washington Street. The site was 12 acres in size, and the building included an auditorium, shops, classrooms, and a gymnasium. Wilson and Roosevelt were built at the same time in Appleton at a cost of $600,000 each. This aerial photograph of Appleton in early winter shows a snow-covered city. (Image courtesy of Carol McIntyre.)

Inspirational teacher Ivan "Ike" Spangenberg directs the Appleton West Band in 1970. This view is from the tuba section in the original school band room. Ike graduated from Appleton High School playing under the direction of Ernest Moore. He continued his education, graduating from Lawrence University. He shared his love for music with students for 38 years in Appleton schools. Tuesday nights, Appleton residents were able to enjoy Appleton City Band under Ike's direction for 40 years. Today, they can still enjoy music directed and played by Ike Spangenberg in area churches. (Image courtesy of Bruce Pollard; caption provided by Kay Forton.)

In 1966, Appleton Area School District put in a new field at Einstein Junior High in honor of Werner Witte. Werner Witte was the longtime athletic director and vice principla of Appleton High School. The crew for Appleton included, faces pictured from left to right, Dave Nobbefeld, Ken Schmidt (superintendent of buildings and grounds), Leroy Borsche, Ervin Steege, Wayne Borsche, and Nate Belling (looking right). The crew worked in every public school in Appleton: on the ceilings, repairing the floors, removing the snow, and more. They were a dedicated group of people who loved Appleton's public schools. (Image courtesy of the Ken Schmidt family.)

Nine

PUBLIC SERVICE
IN WAR AND PEACE

Capt. Maurice S. Peerenboom was commander of Company G, 2nd Regiment of Infantry, Wisconsin National Guard. This photograph was taken at Camp Griffin, Camp Douglas, Wisconsin in 1901. Captain Peerenboom was a first lieutenant under Capt. Hugh Pomeroy of Company G during the Spanish-American War. The bugle player on the right is Frank Schmidt. (Image courtesy of the Ken and Helen Schmidt family.)

The Appleton Fire Department had a rigs steamer to pump water in case of a fire. Here, firemen work on and demonstrate the steamer. Appleton's first volunteer department formed in 1854. The first paid professional department formed in 1894. (Image courtesy of the History Museum at the Castle; caption provided by Brad Brautigam.)

Soldiers of Company G stand in formation in front of Appleton's first armory in 1897, located at the present-day site of the History Museum at the Castle. Built around 1884, this armory would stand for approximately 20 years until Appleton's second armory was erected directly across the street. Many of the men shown in this photograph would participate in the Spanish-American War, fighting in Puerto Rico in 1898. (Caption provided by Joe Gaerthofner)

Spanish-American War veterans marched in this parade in 1898. Appleton participated in the war with Company G of the 2nd Wisconsin Infantry. Out of the 1,352 men in the 2nd Wisconsin Infantry of the Spanish-American War, 111 were from Appleton. The 2nd Wisconsin Infantry was sent to Puerto Rico to hold Ponce and take Coamo. They returned to Appleton in September 1898. The building at the center is Voeck's Meat Market, 716 College Avenue. (Image courtesy of Michael Broeren.)

The post office was located on the corner of Oneida and Washington Streets. The postmen in the 1940s included, from left to right, (first row) Joe Grassberger, Ed Witt, George Grimmer, Bob Schmiege, two unidentified men, Henry Roemer, and Louis Stork; (second row) Hugh Brinkman, Roy Parfilt, Jim Brown, Harry Junge, Wally Horn, Paul Sellin, Joe Roemer, George Weinfurter, and Herman Zschaechnor; (third row) Walter Poetter, John Miller, Bob Shortt, Bob Olson, Ed Campshure, Ed Kirsling, Arwin Frailing, Bill Kositske, and John Letter. (Image courtesy of the Gerhard and Lorraine Junge Vogt family.)

The Appleton Post Office, pictured here around 1912, was located on the west side of Oneida Street between College Avenue and Edwards (now called Washington) Street. This area is currently the inside of the City Center Mall. It was the post office from the 1890s until the early 1920s. According to Ryan's *History of Outagamie County*, "On January 2, 1888, the first free postal delivery occurred in Appleton; one delivery was made that day and three the next and after that several every day." (Image courtesy of John Marx.)

In 1887, Appleton had its first reader room above Pardee's Grocery Store. It was the first free library in Appleton. (Image courtesy of the Appleton Public Library.)

The City of Appleton built a new and grand building for the Appleton Public Library on Oneida Street. On June 1, 1899, the library was formally approved, with Mayor Herman Erb Jr. assessing the swing vote to get it done. The new building finally became reality on March 28, 1900, when it was dedicated and opened. The first floor of the building served as the library; the second floor served as city hall. Horses and wagons were used to bring in the necessary bricks for building. (Image courtesy of Jon Porter.)

In 1869, the City of Appleton approved its first permanent police officer, George Weber. This building housed the police department in 1910. In the image, two young ladies read the news of the day on the board next to the window. (Image courtesy of Arne Nettekoven.)

Members of the Appleton Police Department are pictured in front of the Outagamie County Courthouse in the summer of 1946. The officers on motorbikes (from left to right) included Harry Salzman, Fred Arndt, John Gosch, Marvin Green, Harold Blessman, and Carl Kunitz. (Image courtesy of Arne Nettekoven.)

left to right - 1935 BUICK.
C.Radtke,A.Thomack,Bill Williams.
Chief Prim,A.Deltgen,F.Arndt.

Appleton police officers (left to right) Carl Radtke, A. Thomack, Bill Williams, Chief George Prim, A. Deltgen and F. Arndt stand next to the shiny new 1935 Buick. They are positioned outside of the police station on Midway Street, half a block north of College Avenue between Oneida and Appleton Streets. (Image courtesy of Arne Nettekoven.)

The Appleton Police Department participated in many parades in Appleton. Here, Chief Prim leads a group of officers in a Decoration Day parade. They are followed by a military-style band. The photograph is looking east down College Avenue, toward the armory. (Image courtesy of Arne Nettekoven.)

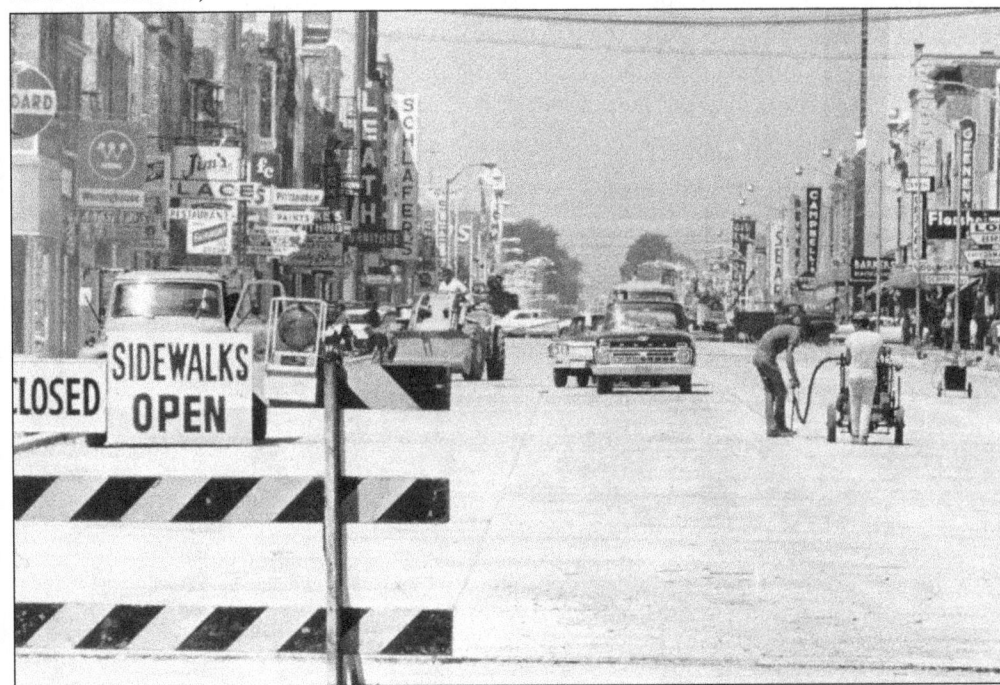

College Avenue was the very first street in Appleton. The early settlers chopped down tree after tree to clear the way. Here, in 1966, Appleton Public Works puts the finishing touches on new pavement for College Avenue. It is a long way removed from the dirty, dusty stumps of 1846. The signs on the avenue include familiar names like Langstadt's, Jim's Place, Leath Furniture, Schlafer's Hardware, Wichman's, Geenen's, Barker's, Campbell's, Sears, and Gloudemans. As the sign says, the sidewalks were always "open." (Image courtesy of Dave Buss.)

The railroad depot at Appleton Street was a popular destination for travelers. It required maintenance to keep up the wooden plank walks that crisscrossed the tracks. Here, workers lay new planks. The men in the railcar are shoveling stone and gravel down to the men below. (Image courtesy of Dave Kalz.)

The electric trolleys ran on tracks through downtown and looped down into the flats. Here, a railroad winter snowplow is used to clear the tracks in downtown Appleton. Behind the snowplow is the B. Douglas building. Byron Douglas was the first dentist in Appleton, and he also worked in real estate. A small sign indicates Hyde and Co's presence in the building. (Image courtesy of Karen Van Lyssel.)

Appleton Water Department workers install a hydrant in front of an area home. The wooden tripod and pulley system steadies the hydrant as they lower it down. (Image courtesy of the Appleton Water Department.)

The Appleton Water Department worked to lay a 12-inch pipe across the Fox River at Lawe Street in 1931. In the background of the photograph, Stephenson Science Hall is on the left and the cupola of Main Hall, on the right. The water department used a crane and several old water pumps to pump out the trench and lay the pipe. (Image courtesy of the Appleton Water Department.)

The City of Appleton Water Works plant was built in 1914 and remained in operation until 2001. The structure treated water from the Fox River to make it drinkable. A swimming pool was added to the plant in the 1920s. (Image courtesy of the Appleton Water Department.)

The Appleton water tower was called the Walnut Street Standpipe when first erected by the city with a bond order in 1914. The tower could hold 500,000 gallons of water. This 1936 photograph shows the freshly painted tower. (Image courtesy of the Appleton Water Department.)

Ten

MUSIC, ART, SPORTS, AND CELEBRATIONS

Baseball was a popular pastime in Appleton. This photograph taken at the Interlake Ball Diamond shows the Noffke's Fuel team. The players are, from left to right, (first row) Paul Grishaber, Clem DeYoung, Clarence Noffke, Wally Noffke, and Frank Kreiss; (second row) coach Ferg "Foxy" Lawrence, Frank Bergman, Earl Kirk, Harry Noffke, Ernie Bergman, Harvey Buss, and Fritz Horn. (Image courtesy of Raymond Noffke.)

Before the Timber Rattlers, or the Appleton Foxes, there were the Appleton Papermakers. They played from 1909 to 1914 and then from 1940 to 1953 on what became known as Goodland Field on West Spencer Street in Appleton. In 1910, the Appleton Papermakers took first place in the Wisconsin-Illinois League. Jack Schwerbel, wearing the black tie, is the only person identified in this c. 1912 photograph. (Image and caption courtesy of Bob Kohl.)

The Appleton Civic Ballet performed *The Enchanted Sea* in 1948. Mrs. Robert Lemke was the director of the ballet, which was performed at Appleton High School. King Neptune was danced by Hannah Rosenthal, and she was accompanied by mermaids Lorrain Vogt, Barbara Hauert, Virginia Blick, Mimi McCorison, and Peggy MacAntamney. (Image courtesy of the Walter and Mickey Schmidt family.)

The Appleton Parks & Recreation Department runs dance programs for the city's children. In 1960, these little ladies performed a tap program on the stage of Appleton High School. The third "I" from the left is Kay Schmidt. (Image courtesy of Kay Forton.)

The 120th Field Artillery Band was first organized in 1917 as the 9th Infantry Band. In 1941, the remnants of the band formed the Appleton City Band. Some early members included George Klein, Peter Heid, and John Brouchek. In 1929, the band competed in the national Elks band contest and took home the first prize. (Images courtesy of Barbara Hirn.)

The Appleton City Band posed for a group photograph in about 1906 in the John Ross Studio. In the first row, the second cornet player from the left is Frank Schmidt, and the third cornet player from the left is John Steidl. Other members of the band, in no particular order, include (additional cornets) Chas. E. Collar, Herm. Bauer, John Hagen, and Geo. Steenis; (clarinets) Lewis Kralls, And. Kraus, Ferd. Lang, John Meyer, Anton Fisher, Geo. Lampert, and Herm. Renfeld; (drums) W. Hassmann, Chas. Lansmann, and Vos Wettengel; (tubas) Henry Bauer, Jos. Humphrey; (baritone) Mat. Bauer; (trombones) Clarence Herrick, Anson Bauer, Lucius Collar, and Frank Humphrey; (alto horns) Jos. Hassman, Will Steenis, Jos. Sommer, and Jos. Guenther; and (drum major) Tony Steffens. (Image courtesy of Ike Spangenberg.)

Ray Brock was the voice of WHBY radio. In 1958, he was the program director running "Appleton's fulltime network of music, news, and sports." Ray delivered the Associated Press newswire and the local news. (Image courtesy of the Koester family.)

WAPL radio personality Bob Bandy hosts a show from the roof of the Balliet Hotel to raise money. The banner says, "Up in the air over youth." The event was a partnership with the Alko Supermarket to raise money for a youth community center. Bob Bandy mounted his tower on July 4, 1958, and was assisted down by the fire department on August 10. (Image courtesy of Dave Buss.)

The Appleton Elk's Club started the United States' longest-running Flag Day parade in 1950. Congress passed an act authorizing June 14 as Flag Day. Many of the Elks had served in World War II and wanted to honor that service. Thousands and thousands of people line the parade route, from Wisconsin Avenue to State Street to College Avenue. There are many businesses lining the street of this photograph, including (right to left) Elm Tree Bakery, Hofensberger Meats, Sherwin-Williams Paints, Shannon's Office Supplies, and more. (Image courtesy of Dave Buss.)

Appleton enjoyed the visits of the traveling circuses. This horse-drawn steam calliope makes its way down College Avenue in about 1900, a bicyclist keeping pace as they glide along. Children watch from the sidewalk and second-floor windows. The businesses on the south side of College Avenue between Durkee and Morrison Streets include tailor John Ross, plumber Henry Nichols, and Cawilk Paint Shop. A large sign advertises for B. Lyons manufacturer of the Capitol Cigar and Quaker Oats. (Image courtesy of Jon Porter.)

The circus brought a menagerie of animals to College Avenue in about 1900. Above, the reindeer, zebras, donkeys, and horses pull the circus delights. The view of College Avenue is looking west past Oneida Street. Boys and girls line the far side of the street with their bicycles, and ladies stand with their sun umbrellas. Below, 24 elephants are on parade, and the street is packed with people catching a glimpse of the sights. (Above image courtesy of the Ken Weiland family; below image courtesy of the Tom Butler family.)

Appleton held a parade to send off the soldiers to World War I. Above, the 120th Field Artillery Band plays as they march past the Globe Hotel and Welcome Hyde home. Below, the soldiers pass by. Welcome Hyde was an influential real estate dealer in Appleton. He was involved in developing a considerable part of west Appleton, and he named two streets after his sons DeForest and Lafayette. The streets were renamed Spring and Summer. (Images courtesy of Gretchen Hauert.)

Visit us at
arcadiapublishing.com

www.ingramcontent.com/pod-product-compliance
Lightning Source LLC
Chambersburg PA
CBHW080549110426
42813CB00006B/1257